THE MAD CRUSH

A Memoir of Mythic Vines and Improbable Winemaking

SEAN CHRISTOPHER WEIR

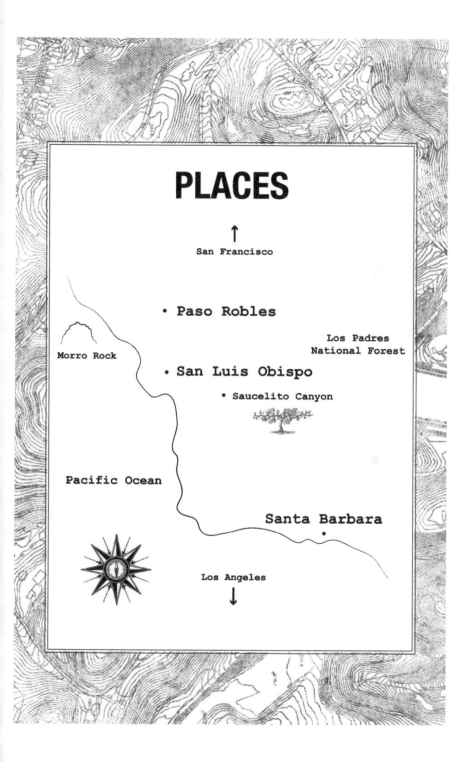

Published by Mooncatcher Media

Cover design by Stefanie Collins
Back cover photo by Chris Leschinsky
Interior layout by Adina Cucicov at Flamingo Designs

ISBN: 978-0-9851579-4-4

The first time Bill made wine,
he was buck naked...

CONTENTS

PROLOGUE

THE BOTTLE WAS retrieved from an earthen cellar chiseled into the hillside. It was flecked with dirt, and the label was jagged at the edges. But the time and the place and the grape variety were still legible: 1995 Saucelito Canyon Zinfandel.

The 1995 vintage wasn't the only wine retrieved from the cave on this July evening. Out came other dusty remnants of years past. Corks were carefully pulled, and a line formed to taste the old wines.

The occasion was the 35th anniversary of Bill Greenough's first day spent here as the owner of Rancho Saucelito, where he had restored a century-old vineyard by himself, armed with a pick and shovel.

More than 100 people, mainly family, friends and wine club members, had come to celebrate the man, and to enjoy a retrospective tasting of the wines of Saucelito Canyon Vineyard.

In the adjacent winery, the latest vintage remained in the barrel. The next vintage was still hanging out on the nearby vines, confined to little green pellets that would become fat, juicy grapes over the next eight weeks.

The place looked different yet familiar to me. Some of the rough edges had been polished. The lawn was greener, the paint on the winery was brighter. But by nightfall, after the crowd was gone and when the coyotes started howling, I was sure that Saucelito Canyon would feel largely unchanged.

Despite the many wines being poured that evening, I only had eyes for the 1995 vintage. It was a wine that I had helped make, and that I hadn't tasted in more than a dozen years. I watched intently as the server dusted off the bottle, and I flinched a bit when the corkscrew penetrated the cork. In some ways, that seal was sacred to me. Now it was broken.

I watched as the wine tumbled into the glass, deep purple at its core, but bronzed by age at the ridges. And as I worked up the nerve to tilt my nose to the glass, I wondered: Could this wine still speak to the 1995 harvest? Or had it turned to vinegar, leaving no evidence of the escapades that it had inspired once upon a time?

While working that now-distant harvest, I'd discovered that the true romance of winemaking was the process itself, the act of physically willing mere grapes to become something infinitely more beautiful, and more lasting. Left to their own devices, grapes will just rot. But when turned into wine, they tell a story.

This is the story of the 1995 Saucelito Canyon Zinfandel, and of those who made it.

Chapter One

THE CALLING

THE PHONE RANG on a random afternoon in late July of 1995. I was surprised to hear Bill Greenough's voice at the other end of the line. I hadn't talked to him in more than a year.

"I need your help," he said. "I'm wondering if you would come down and work the crush for me."

Bill had been grinding away at Saucelito Canyon for the past two decades, and now another harvest was around the corner, and so was another "crush"—the seasonal push to process the harvested fruit and turn it into wine.

Bill would usually hire some local college kids to work the crush and leave it at that. In fact, I had been one of his part-time student hires three years earlier. But now he said that he wanted to enlist someone with experience, someone he could trust to be there day and night to help lighten his load. He sounded burned out. I'd never heard him like that. I knew he'd gone through some things recently, but I didn't probe. Bill was a man of few words. He wasn't the type to share his troubles.

"When would you need me to start?" I asked.

"It's up to you, but it would be nice if you could get here by late August to help ramp things up," he said, adding that I could stay in the unoccupied cottage house he'd built next to the winery many years ago.

I told him I'd think about it, but my decision had essentially been made. I just needed a little more time to consider the ramifications of uprooting myself and committing to another crush.

There wasn't much to uproot. I was living in a studio apartment beneath the house of my landlord. My apartment consisted of a small room with a walk-in closet. I slept in the closet.

Three years earlier, I had graduated from college. Now I was putting my journalism degree to use as a waiter for a catering company. All of my worldly possessions, as I would soon find out, could fit in the back of my little Mitsubishi pickup truck. My cat would ride shotgun.

What Bill didn't know, and what I didn't figure out until years later, was that on that fateful summer day in 1995, I needed him just as much as he needed me.

Bill moved to Saucelito Canyon on July 4, 1974, his first official day as the owner of the old Rancho Saucelito. He had
come from Santa Barbara hauling two horses, two dogs,
one cat and a last load of furniture with his red Ford truck.

The canyon was located in the upper Arroyo Grande
Valley at the edge of the Los Padres National Forest in San
Luis Obispo County, in the heart of California's Central
Coast. To the west of the canyon, about 18 miles away, was
the Pacific Ocean. To the immediate east was pure wilderness. Saucelito Canyon was on the edge of civilization. If
you wanted to declare your independence, this was the
place to do it.

When Bill arrived, Saucelito Canyon didn't look much
different than it did back in 1880, when an English expa-
triate named Henry Ditmas planted the three acres of Zinfandel vines that would soon become the center of Bill's
universe.

Bill could see what must have attracted Mr. Ditmas to
the canyon. Yes, it was rough and remote, but there was
also something vaguely mystical about it, about the way
the landforms merged here, as if pointing to something. It
was a place that begged to be discovered, and to be settled
by hardy souls.

Looking northward, the canyon walls converged and

then dipped into a notch on the far horizon. From this notch rose the vertical stone edifice of Hi Mountain, a sight both majestic and incongruous. At sunset, wisps of coastal clouds would encircle the mountain, casting upon it a glow of crimson, orange, amber and violet.

This sunset silhouette was so striking that Bill later chose to depict it on the label of each bottle of Saucelito Canyon Zinfandel, a testament to the wine's most important ingredient: place.

Henry Ditmas came to Saucelito Canyon in a horse-drawn carriage in the late 1870s. He had previously made his living as a sheep herder in the Carrizo Plains and as a grocer in Avila Beach. He was 6,000 miles away from his homeland of Great Britain.

Bill, on the other hand, was a fugitive from the waning 1960s Age of Aquarius who had grown up just 80 miles down the road in the moneyed hamlet of Montecito, amid the swaying palms and golden beaches of America's Riviera, as the Santa Barbara coastline was known.

On paper, these men couldn't have been more different. But in reality, they had much in common. Both were seekers, dreamers and adventurers who had other options, but who chose this place, Saucelito Canyon, to put down roots. Both were hard workers who preferred to toil outside with their boots in the dirt. Both loved the process of growing and making wine, the seasons in the vineyard, and the perennial promise that the skeletal vines of the new year would, in a mere nine months, burst forth with fruit and yield vats full of warm, frothy wine.

Ditmas had planted Zinfandel and Muscat vines as well as apple and pear trees. He and his wife Rosa made wine and carved out a comfortable life in the canyon. If this were a storybook, Henry and Rosa would have grown old together, sipping wine in rocking chairs, watching the sunsets explode over Hi Mountain.

Instead, they got divorced in 1886. Henry moved away to San Francisco, then Boston, and died of pneumonia in 1892. Rosa stayed behind and married neighboring rancher A.B. Hasbrouck, who had established his own vineyard and winery called St. Remy. Rosa and her new husband continued to run Rancho Saucelito as well.

A sustained drought in the early 1900s put St. Remy out of business—the vines died right along with the cows. However, the vineyard and winemaking operations at Rancho Saucelito survived. The official records are scant, but the oral history has Rosa leasing the property to the police chief of Guadalupe, a coastal town south of Arroyo Grande. The police chief would bring his convicts out to the canyon for vineyard labor. Local cowboys would come out to the vineyard on the weekend to drink and dance, and legend has it that they enjoyed themselves so much that they weren't worth a damn until Tuesday.

The property was later leased to a colorful Italian-American winemaker. His foreman worked all week under the stipulation that he could drink as much as he wanted on the weekends. But then Prohibition was enacted, and the Feds came out to the canyon, rolled the barrels out of the winery and started splitting them open with hatchets. Red wine was running like a river down the dirt road. The foreman grabbed a shovel and started making a dam out of the dirt, creating a little pool of wine. He then got on his hands and knees and starting slurping the wine up off the ground, all the while screaming at the "sons-a-bitches" who were wasting his grog. Bill heard that story from multiple sources.

The winery was later allowed to produce wine for sacramental purposes. The wine was hauled out to Port San Luis, loaded onto boats and shipped up the coast.

Eventually, Rosa, now widowed, leased the Rancho Saucelito property to other tenants who continued to tend the vines until the late 1940s. A surviving newspaper advertisement from that time pitches Saucelito Canyon wine for 50 cents per gallon, with the condition of "bring your own container."

In time, however, the vineyard operations ceased. The property was subsequently used for dryland grazing.

The glory days were over. Rancho Saucelito was abandoned, and soon the vineyard became a scrubby mirage of its once vibrant self.

⸎

Bill discovered Henry Ditmas's old vines during his first visit to the canyon in 1974 as a prospective buyer of the old Rancho Saucelito—so named for the property's little willow trees, called *sauce* in Spanish.

The vineyard wasn't much to look at when he arrived, just a grid of gnarled stumps ensnared in dry brush and poison oak. If he wanted to grow grapes here, he figured that he'd have to rip the stumps out and start anew.

The vines were widely spaced at eight feet apart so that the vineyard could be farmed by horse and plow. The exposed vines looked dead, devoid of vegetation. Others were completely overgrown by the brush.

But then Bill took a closer look. He approached one of the shrouded vines and pulled the scrubby curtain back. What he saw blew his mind—little grape clusters, protected from the hungry wildlife by the thick overgrowth.

The vineyard wasn't as dead as it looked. In fact, to the careful eye, it was still quite alive. Bill was suddenly struck by a crazy thought—*instead of removing these old vines, what if I could restore them?*

And so it came to be that under the hot autumn sun of

1974, Bill went to work, hacking his way through the overgrowth. Slowly but surely, he uncovered Henry Ditmas's vineyard, vine by vine. That was the easy part.

Next, he dug into the root zone of each vine, searching for fresh growth. Yes, the vines were alive, but their gnarled crowns were no longer functional for winegrowing. Bill selected the strongest fresh shoot from each root zone and trained it upward. From these shoots a new crown would be born, and an old vineyard would thrive again, its tired roots reinvigorated by the fresh growth and supercharged by the resulting photosynthesis.

Before Bill arrived, the vines could only struggle to survive. Now he had reawakened them, and they would soon return the favor by yielding some of California's most remarkable Zinfandel.

⁀ᛦ⁀

Bill would later plant additional blocks of Zinfandel, but the wine that came from the old vines was different than the others. It was wiser, more nuanced, and less exuberant than the wine from the younger vines. You could almost taste the dusty canyon soil percolating through the fruit. There was a sense that the old vines had gone native over the preceding 100 years, that they'd become almost indigenous to the property, as much a legitimate part of the landscape as the scrub oak and mountain lions.

In time, Bill developed a personal relationship with the vines. On evenings leading up to the harvest, after we had called it quits for the day, I would see him walking the vineyard in the diminishing light, tasting the grapes, watchful and engaged.

This was Bill in his element, listening to the vines, reading the fruit, seeking clues and signals and signs. The vines were his babies. Just as parents are finely tuned to the slightest expression or gesture from their children, Bill was uniquely able to decipher the state of his vines. The numbers in the lab may have said the fruit was ready to pick. Fine. But was it truly time, or did the vines want just one more day, or two more days? Only Bill knew the answer.

Bill's viticultural intuition had been forged over two decades and countless hours prowling this ten-acre slice of isolation. He knew exactly where the clay loam soil transitioned to sandy loam, and how the vines reacted to the difference. He knew the spots where rainwater pooled, and the spots where it would drain like a sieve. He knew the shadier spots and the sunnier spots and how to farm them accordingly.

To Bill, the vineyard wasn't a plot of land. It was a jigsaw puzzle, a mosaic of little pieces, each with its own curves and bevels and quirks. He approached these pieces with respect and discernment.

There was also a larger environmental context to the vineyard. Saucelito Canyon occupied a chaparral ecosystem.

Chaparral is defined as a shrubby coastal terrain shaped by warm, dry summers and mild winters. The word comes from *chaparro*, which means scrub oak in Spanish. Manzanita, ceanothus and chamise are among the other plant species that populate the chaparral community. Chaparral is a sort of organic gasoline, fueling many of California's frequent wildfires, often with the warm autumn Santa Ana winds as a willing accomplice. Modern fire suppression efforts and management techniques such as prescribed burns have proven to be futile in chaparral country, if not counterproductive. The devil always gets his due.

Bill grew up in the coastal chaparral, and had witnessed its explosiveness firsthand. In 1964, a wildfire tore through the Santa Barbara mountains, burning virtually everything in its path, but somehow sparing the Greenough residence. The family lawnmower, however, was turned into a stream of liquid metal.

The chaparral was in Bill's blood, and it was one of the things that initially attracted him to Saucelito Canyon, this sense of a familiar ecosystem. He also understood that the coastal chaparral was not only a terrific firestarter, but also a great place to grow grapes.

Indeed, the conditions that defined the local chaparral—dry summers, reliable marine breezes and rocky, nutrient-starved soils—were also the architecture of world-class wine.

Chapter Two

HOMECOMING

ON AUGUST 18, 1995, I found my way back to Saucelito Canyon. The allure of another crush had proven too hard to resist, and I had accepted Bill's invitation.

When I arrived, Bill greeted me like I had never left, which is to say that he barely greeted me. There was work to be done, after all. Thankfully, I knew my way around the place, having worked the crush there three years earlier.

I unloaded my truck and put everything in the cottage, and spent the rest of the afternoon getting oriented to the tasks at hand. The grapes were still weeks away from being picked.

For the layperson, here's how red wine is made: You grow grapes until they are sweet, then you pick them off the vine and crush them in a container while removing the stems, leaving you with a mass of skins, seeds, pulp and juice. You add yeast to the mass, which ferments the grape sugars into alcohol and carbon dioxide gas. The gas blows off. You strain the liquid away from the skins and seeds, and voila, you've got wine.

Making wine is easy. You could do it in your bathtub. But making drinkable wine? That's not so easy. As for making great wine, well, that's a pain in the ass.

Bill didn't give me a master plan for the crush, but he gave me assignments and talked about what needed to be done, and I had just enough experience to fill in the blanks. The road map at Saucelito Canyon looked something like this:

Preparation

Clean and prepare all equipment—crusher-destemmer, pumps and hoses, fermentation bins and tanks, winery floors and walls (half of winemaking is glorified janitorial work).

Controls

Keep birds, deer and yellowjackets from helping themselves to the grape buffet; sprinkle the adjacent dirt driveway with water on breezy days to keep dust from coating the vines with grime and harmful dust-borne mites.

Filtration and Bottling

Empty the winery barrels of the previous vintage to make room for the new one; transfer the wine to tanks, filter the wine to remove solids, and bottle the wine on site with a mobile bottling line.

Pick Grapes

Different parts of the vineyard typically reach peak ripeness on different days, and the picking crews respond accordingly; staggered ripeness is a good thing, because there is simply no way to pick and process all of the vineyard's fruit at once.

Sort and Process Grapes

Sort the clusters by hand, discarding any rotten or unripe fruit, as well as leaves and debris; de-stem and lightly crush the grapes in the crusher-destemmer, then move them into fermentation bins and tanks.

Fermentation

Add commercial winemaking yeasts to initiate fermentation. During fermentation, the wine can get very warm, and if it gets too warm, the yeasts can shut down, and you will end up with a "stuck" fermentation. Not good.

Punchdowns

As fermentation proceeds, the gaseous bubbling of the liquid pushes the grape skins to the top of the bin or tank, forming a cap that can quickly dry out; because grape skins are essential for imparting color, flavor and tannin to the wine, the cap must be manually broken up and punched down into the liquid with a long paddle. This process is not unlike pushing a tea bag back down into the hot water to get more color and flavor.

Pressing

At the conclusion of fermentation, much of the new wine runs free from the tank, but quite a bit of liquid still remains suspended in the pulpy mass of leftover skins; the skins must be manually shoveled out of the tank or bin and dumped into a press; lightly pressing the skins releases the remainder of the wine.

Barreling Down

The free-run wine and pressed wine are transferred to tanks for settling, then to barrels to begin the aging process; all of the various messes are cleaned up and the crush equipment is placed in storage, and another vintage is put to bed.

On paper, the crush always looked like a breeze. But in practice, it never was.

My winemaking "career" had begun on a painful note four years earlier at Kenwood Vineyards in the Sonoma Valley.

I was securing a hose to a tank high above the crush pad in preparation for the 1991 harvest. The hose was bent into a tight corner when it slipped out of my hands, its tension releasing with startling velocity. It was a rookie mistake. The metal fitting at the end of the hose exploded right through two front teeth, leaving me dazed and concussed with a mouthful of bony grit.

After an emergency visit to the dentist and an afternoon recovering on the couch, I returned to the job. My official title was "cellar rat," and it entitled me to work like a dog with barely a day off for the ensuing two months.

That first harvest job at Kenwood Vineyards was the culmination of things.

I grew up in the town of Sonoma, back when it still put the "country" in wine country. The backroads near my house were speckled with humble little vineyards. In Little League, I played against teams sponsored by Sebastiani and Parducci wineries. Wine wasn't anything too special back then. It was just a local way of life.

I went to high school in Napa, and as I grew older, I became increasingly drawn to the wine industry. I worked in the restaurant at Domaine Chandon as a back waiter when I was 20 years old. The general manager at the time, Daniel Shanks, went on to become the sommelier at the White House. The chef, Philippe Jeanty, would later establish his own highly regarded namesake bistro. If you allowed a sparkling wine cork to make a loud pop in the dining room, they would kick your butt when you got back in the kitchen. It was wine, food and hospitality at a level I'd never seen before.

From there, I headed down to San Luis Obispo to finish college at Cal Poly, and I got a weekend job pouring wine at the Chamisal Vineyard tasting room. I also did a little cellar work for Chamisal's winemaker Clay Thompson, who operated his own little winery, Claiborne & Churchill Vintners, behind a roll-up door in a small industrial park. Clay entrusted me with various tasks, such as racking wine and topping up the barrels. I was getting the wine bug. By the end of the summer of 1991, I only had one more quarter of classes left to earn my degree, but I decided to postpone my education in favor of working the harvest that fall.

I sent out my resume to several wineries on the Central Coast and back home in the Sonoma Valley. Kenwood Vineyards answered the call, largely due to a personal connection. My father was a telephone man, and he had installed the phone systems at the winery. Kenwood Vineyards was owned by winemaker Mike Lee and his brother Marty Lee, along with their brother-in-law John Sheela.

They knew and liked my father, who had passed away from a heart attack a year and a half earlier—a total blindside hit, as he had exhibited no health problems. Mike Lee decided to give his son a shot.

My main task was hauling grapes to the winery in a two-wheel "gondola" trailer hitched to the back of a pickup truck. I was a greenhorn college kid who'd never driven a truck or hitched a trailer. I didn't know what I was doing at first. But I got the hang of it and soon enough I was maneuvering the rig through tight vineyard spots and back to the winery.

The job was harrowing at times, due to the fact that the payload was far heavier than the vehicle. Sometimes while I was navigating the curves on Highway 12, the gondola would start swaying, yanking the rear end of the truck back and forth, as if ready to whip it around and create a holy grape mess. In fact, toward the end of harvest, it happened to one of our guys. Thankfully, his gondola detached and didn't take the truck with it before spinning off into the ditch amid a hailstorm of flying fruit.

There was also the story of the guy who forgot to secure an empty gondola to the back of his truck before driving away from the crusher. As he descended down the driveway, the gondola detached and smashed through the wall of the tasting room. So I learned to drive slowly and triple-check the hitch.

When I wasn't hauling grapes, I was working in the cellar, filling barrels, washing barrels, shoveling grape skins, pumping wine and cleaning tanks. The hours were brutal, the days off were few. I was a little starry eyed at the start of harvest, driven by the more romantic notions of winemaking. But by the end, I was more punch drunk than starry eyed. When we were working on something particularly mundane, such as scrubbing the concrete floors or hauling hoses, someone would inevitably cry out, "*Now* we're making wine!"

Kenwood Vineyards was a big winery, but there was still a strong family vibe running through it. When the harvest was in full swing, the non-cellar employees were tasked with creating festive lunches. Then, in the early afternoon, we would all sit around picnic tables in the shade, attacking the food and enjoying wine. Everyone drank responsibly, never exceeding a glass.

One of my favorite moments of the harvest came at the crack of dawn one morning when I arrived at Milo Shepard's Jack London Vineyard, named after the famous author who had made his home on the surrounding ranch in the early 1900s. Milo was a descendent of Jack London, and he had planted the vineyard starting in 1973. When I was a little boy, my dad would take me up to the adjacent Jack London State Park, where we would walk the wooded trails and keep an eye out for blue-belly lizards.

As I sat waiting for the grapes to roll in from Milo's vineyard that morning, I fondly recalled those moments with my dad. I sure missed him. The sun was just rising, and despite the undercurrent of grief, Jack London himself took the words right out of my mouth with the famous line from his autobiographical novel *John Barleycorn*: "The grapes on a score of rolling hills are red with autumn flame. Across Sonoma Mountain, wisps of sea fog are stealing...I have everything to make me glad I am alive."

In time, the days began to blend together under the warm Sonoma sun. The lunches were the only true respite in a blur of long shifts followed by a quick shower and dinner. At the crack of dawn, the alarm would ring, and the blur would pick up where it left off. The harvest was a grind, but a happy grind. By the end of it, I was far from a "winemaker," but I now understood what went into making wine.

☙

By the following autumn, in 1992, I was ready for more. That's how I first found my way to Saucelito Canyon.

I'd stayed on at Kenwood Vineyards through the spring, then spent the summer taking a poor man's tour of France and Italy. Now it was time to finish my degree, so I returned to Cal Poly for the fall quarter.

On the job board at the university, I saw that a local winery called Saucelito Canyon Vineyard needed some help with the harvest. I made the call, and Bill Greenough answered the phone. He identified himself as the owner. He mumbled a few details about the job. I told him that I'd worked in some local tasting rooms, and that I'd also worked the previous crush at Kenwood Vineyards. That was good enough for him. He gave me directions and said I could start working the next day.

The directions seemed reasonable enough on paper, but about halfway through the drive I started to wonder what I'd gotten myself into.

About seven miles south of San Luis Obispo, I turned eastward onto Lopez Drive, traveling another several miles to Lopez Lake tucked into the increasingly remote hills.

From there, I took a winding road deeper into the wilds until I saw the gate Bill had told me about. I used the combination he'd given me to open the lock. I continued along a pitted dirt road, dodging a few tarantulas along the way.

The canyon began to narrow. To the right, a looming scrub-studded mesa paralleled the road, walling off the western view. On the opposite side of the canyon, the rolling terrain was less imposing, but no less rugged. Civilization was now well behind me, further obscured by the plumes of dust stoked by my tires. Ahead, the dirt road stretched into the far horizon and looked like it might never end.

Bill had told me that the vineyard was out in the country. He hadn't told me that it was in the middle of nowhere.

Saucelito Canyon was tucked into the ripples of ancient seismic unrest, where the terrain had buckled into jagged mountain ranges amid the relentless grinding of the Pacific plate against the North American plate. The mighty San Andreas Fault paralleled the nearby coastline, slicing through the Carrizo Plain approximately 50 miles east of the canyon.

The postal address of the winery was Arroyo Grande, the small coastal town 16 miles to the west. It was a long 16 miles, as the trek began or ended—depending on whether you were coming or going—with the pitted dirt of Saucelito Creek Road and the twisting turns of Hi Mountain Road.

The route from the canyon to town took you through the Arroyo Grande Valley. The canyon was located in the "upper" valley. The lower valley terminated at the ocean. The Arroyo Grande Valley and the adjacent Edna Valley were the two winegrowing areas of southern San Luis Obispo County, a region collectively known as San Luis Obispo Wine Country. A third winegrowing appellation, Paso Robles, spanned the northern part of the county.

San Luis Obispo County was the geographical epicenter of the Central Coast. The town of Atascadero, in the geographical middle of the county, was 215 miles from San Francisco to the north and 218 miles from Los Angeles to the south. The county was also fairly equidistant from Monterey to the north, Santa Barbara to the south, Fresno to the northeast, and Bakersfield to the east. Such symmetrical distance from California's urban landmarks was largely responsible for preserving the area's rural identity and relative isolation. Unlike the Sonoma and Napa wine countries, which were in the Bay Area's backyard, San Luis Obispo County couldn't be easily overrun by urban refugees.

The county seat was the college town of San Luis Obispo. San Luis Obispo was part of California's famed mission trail. Father Junipero Serra founded Mission San Luis Obispo de Tolosa in 1772, and the mission remained a centerpiece of the downtown. In the late 1770s, the padres established an *asistencia*, or assistance mission, eight miles northeast of San Luis Obispo at the top of the Cuesta Grade, on what is now known as Santa Margarita Ranch. There, they raised cattle and grew grapes for sacramental wine.

Continuing northward from San Luis Obispo, you could head further inland along Highway 101 and into Paso Robles, or take the Pacific Coast Highway along the coast to Morro Bay, Cambria, Hearst Castle and, eventually, the Big Sur coastline.

Morro Bay was an eccentric fishing town with an industrial backdrop. Three 450-foot smokestacks rose up from a waterfront power plant and loomed over the bay. But an even more impressive object dwarfed the smokestacks and defined the skyline: Morro Rock. This barren dome rose out of the bay at a height of 581 feet, never failing to drop the jaws of first-time visitors.

Morro Rock was the most dramatic member of a chain of peaks known as the Seven Sisters—although some counted two additional formations and called them the Nine Sisters. These unique rounded peaks, called morros, were the remnant plugs of extinct volcanoes, and they cut across the county in a linear southeastern path from Morro Bay through San Luis Obispo. The sisters terminated at Islay Hill amid the vineyards in Edna Valley, just a few miles from the Arroyo Grande Valley and the road that led to Saucelito Canyon.

The Seven Sisters were the most visible testament to the molten unrest and unrelenting friction that ultimately forged the unique *terroir*—a French word that roughly translates to "sense of place"—of the local viticultural landscape.

Terroir is largely defined by the interplay of soil and climate. In a terrain as contorted and complex as San Luis Obispo County, this interplay was often dramatically different from one vineyard to the next. Saucelito Canyon was a textbook example of terroir in action: an isolated vineyard, where the grapes, and therefore the wine, couldn't help but reflect the specific personality of their place.

Standing on the ridge behind the winery, overlooking

the canyon, you had to appreciate what the millennia had wrought—the sharp-edged mesa in the foreground and the stone edifice of Hi Mountain commanding the horizon, and then the gentler coastal folds in the distance as you looked west toward the Pacific Ocean.

It was humbling to consider the geologic violence that had been required to create such a scene. Equally remarkable was the fact that it wasn't uncommon to discover marine fossils percolating through the soil at Saucelito Canyon. The vineyard was situated at 800 feet above sea level and 18 miles from the beach. But once upon a time, the land had been undersea. In some ways, the wine made here was millions of years in the making.

After traveling one and a half miles down the tooth-rattling dirtway of Saucelito Creek Road, just when I thought I might be lost, I found the vineyard. It was tucked behind a curtain of oaks and willows, and cradled by mountainous slopes.

Bill came out to greet me. He wore a bushy mustache that was neatly groomed. His hair stood in stark contrast, uncombed and unruly. His jeans and boots were stained purple with wine. He struggled to make eye contact, and he spoke with a mumbling cadence.

"You know much about wine?" he asked.

He'd apparently forgotten what I told him on the phone.

"Yeah, I worked the crush last year," I said. "But I'm rusty."

He led me on a brief tour of the operation, and five minutes later I found myself shoveling grape skins out of a fermentation tank.

In time, I got the lay of the land. The vineyard was shaped like a boot, with the toe pointing southeast, cradled by the ascending scrub forest. At the heel of the boot was the small winery building, which consisted of a cellar and a tiny lab with a counter and sink.

The back of the winery opened up to a narrow concrete crushpad. The combined footprint of the winery and crushpad was no larger than a small house. Behind the winery and up the hill was a pole barn, which stored a tractor, hardware, tools, scrap metal, riding lawnmower, old motorcycles, a shotgun-shell reloader and the carcass of a vintage sports car, among other things.

Next to the winery was a lawn shaded by a large oak tree. Near the lawn was a small cave carved out of the hillside. The cave dated back to the 19th century. It was sealed with a heavy wooden door. This is where Bill stashed his library of older vintages, as well as a few precious bottles of "seep"—whiskey that had seeped out of some retired spirits barrels he'd purchased years ago for aging wine. The barrels were dry when they'd been shipped from the distillery located somewhere in the American South. By the time they arrived in the canyon, however, pure oak-filtered whiskey had seeped from the pores of the wood and was sloshing around in the bottoms of the barrels. Bill had funneled the whiskey into bottles and corked them.

On the other side of the lawn was the small cottage that Bill had built 20 years earlier. It was unoccupied, but used occasionally when someone needed to crash. It was built into the hillside, with stilts supporting the front rooms. The cottage was shaded by great oaks, and the porch offered wide-open views of the vineyard below and the endless chaparral beyond. As far as the eye could see, except for the winery and the vines, there was no further evidence of mankind.

During the 1992 harvest, I got schooled in what Bill and his wife Nancy called "the Saucelito Way." As they were fond of saying, "There's the right way, the wrong way, and then there's the Saucelito Way."

The Saucelito Way was a revelation to me. I'd cut my teeth at a modern winery stocked with the latest winemaking equipment. By comparison, the crusher and other equipment at Saucelito Canyon were almost toy-like, about one step removed from home winemaking gear. My winemaking world had been turned upside down.

There was stuff that went on here that would keep an enology professor up at night. There was too much of some things (the primary fermentations were too hot, the barrels were too old, the secondary fermentations were too long) and too little of other things (the press was too small, the electricity was too unreliable). Bill was a self-taught wine-maker, and he relied as much on intuition as he did on technical considerations.

Yet the wines were really good, and Saucelito Canyon had earned a reputation as one of California's premier Zinfandel producers. And so my eyes were opened to an entirely different way of doing things, and the more time I spent in the canyon, the more I began to understand wine as something personal and soulful. The winemaking text-books weren't wrong—they just couldn't fully account for a place like this.

I was a part-timer that fall. I hauled buckets, cleaned tanks, filled barrels and ran errands. As the 1992 harvest unfolded, I began to enjoy the long drive out to the canyon, from the busy streets of San Luis Obispo, past the gentle rolling vineyards of the Edna Valley, and, finally, into this other world, this harsh yet beautiful place where nothing else mattered but the wine.

One evening, when it was just Bill and me finishing up, I got up the nerve to ask him why he did it. It was a loaded question: why did he bother with restoring an old vineyard; why did he put himself through the annual trials of the harvest; why did he choose to spend so many lonely days out here riding the tractor and topping the barrels; and why did he put up with having to make it all work in this faraway place with no irrigation or power lines?

He paused for a moment, then said quietly, "Because it must be done."

I was taken aback, and didn't know what to say. It was a weird answer. I was expecting something more explanatory. But the more I thought about it, the more it made sense. In his own way, he was telling me that it was more of a calling than a choice.

Bill and I didn't become particularly close during my first tour of duty in the canyon. In fact, we rarely talked about anything besides the job at hand. He would mumble some idea or directive, and off I would go.

Nevertheless, a vague connection seemed to develop between us. I think it was as simple as the fact that we trusted each other. We vowed to stay in touch, but we really didn't, and I never dreamed that I would be back in the canyon three years later.

⌒◠◠)

At the time, I never considered Bill a father figure. I only came to that realization many years later.

I was book smart when I arrived at Saucelito Canyon, but Bill taught me to think with my hands. He led by example. Self reliance, hard work and personal responsibility were his totems. The crush lasted less than two months, but I learned things that would last a lifetime.

I never once saw Bill lose his cool under pressure. He cursed under his breath on occasion, but that was about it. If you screwed up, he didn't verbally express his disappointment or disapproval. He just gave you a quick and telling look, almost like he pitied you. It was fatherly, and effective.

After finishing my first crush at Saucelito Canyon and earning my degree, I returned home to work as a hospitality coordinator for a winery in Napa. The place was overrun with corporate incompetence, and I eventually walked out the door. I didn't have another job waiting for me, nor did I have a plan. I was beginning to flail around and lose my bearings. I didn't become a drug addict or a vagrant. It was just a slow drift, destination unknown.

I moved down to Santa Cruz County, where I did some odd jobs and eventually found steady work with a catering company. My catering colleagues were a merry band of seekers, misfits and old timers, and I loved them.

Working special events and private dinners for wealthy clients on Monterey Bay was routinely amusing. One wealthy wannabe "rancher" client got pissed when we served meat chili instead of vegetarian chili, because it was supposedly giving bad vibes to her trophy cows. Some clients seemed to really enjoy showing us around their lavish homes, always leaving me wondering why they felt the need to impress a bunch of indigent waiters. A few clients were absurdly imperious, while others were unfailingly gracious. I was having a blast.

But Santa Cruz can be a place where ambition goes to die. Don't get me wrong, it's a wonderful place, but it's also very easy to get comfortable with the status quo there, to get lulled by the fun and the mild weather and endless beaches, and by the gravitational pull of the Surf City counterculture.

My first housemate in the area was a 40-year-old cook who worked the dinner shift. He would come home at night and, like clockwork, smoke a fat joint. He listened exclusively to reggae music, all the time. He surfed every morning for hours. He never wavered from his routine. He was the fittest 40-year-old pothead I'd ever seen. On paper, such a life might sound attractive to someone stuck in a cubicle. Who wouldn't want to surf every day, beholden to no one, physically fit and comfortably stoned? But trust me, it wasn't as happy as it sounds.

After two years in the area, I was working hard, but going nowhere. The worst part was that I didn't really care. I was becoming one of the many aimless moons orbiting the enabling sun of Santa Cruz.

What I needed was a swift kick in the ass. A change in trajectory. A new latitude. And I got all of those things at once when Bill called out of the blue and asked if I would help with the 1995 harvest.

I went from sleeping in and working late to getting up at the crack of dawn and still working late. I ditched the waiter's bowtie for work boots. I left the lazy beaches for the prickly chaparral. I stopped living in my own little world and started living in Bill's little world. Residing and working in the wildlands of Saucelito Canyon was its own form of boot camp. I found it invigorating, even purifying.

It was like giving a lost man a compass. I was no longer running in place. The crush put fresh wind in my sails.

Chapter Three

REBELLION

THE FIRST TIME Bill made wine, he was buck naked. Clothing wasn't optional at the communal grape stompings on Mountain Drive above Santa Barbara. It was forbidden.

"You could wear a hat, but that was about it," Bill said.

So there he found himself, in a five-foot diameter vat, literally hanging out with other naked women and men, their arms locked as they stomped the fruit and whooped it up. The year was 1968.

Bill had moved to Mountain Drive in the spring. He came from nearby Montecito, a wealthy enclave just south of Santa Barbara. He was newly married. He had a friend who lived on Mountain Drive, and Bill had always admired his friend's adobe house. Bill also liked the rambunctious, eccentric ambiance of the neighborhood, which was in direct contrast to the one he had grown up in.

When the friend told him he was moving to Mexico and was putting the house up for sale, Bill asked him his price. He said $27,500. Bill countered with an offer of $30,000, to include the house and the Ferrari Spider that was in the garage. His friend accepted, and handed over the keys to the house and the car.

Mountain Drive wasn't just a neighborhood. It was a countercultural outpost populated by artists, writers, builders, potters, performers and other assorted free spirits.

In his book *Mountain Drive: Santa Barbara's Pioneer Bohemian Community*, local historian Elias Chiacos wrote, "The beginnings of the hot-tubbing phenomenon, the Renaissance Faire, the revival of early music, crafts and pageantry—all mounted with a rowdy humor and uninhibited sexuality—hallmark Mountain Drive's contribution to the California dream."

The roots of the Mountain Drive community can be traced back to a local freethinker named Bobby Hyde. According to Chiacos, "Everyone seems to agree that Bobby Hyde, born in 1900, a writer and son of a Santa Barbara artist, instigated the plan to create the community based on his desire to live an unconventional life, close to the land, and in the company of those of like mind. To this end, he and his wife Florence, widely known as Floppy, purchased 50 acres of rugged, fire-blackened land in the hills above Santa Barbara. They proceeded to parcel it out by the acre to relatives and new-found friends in the postwar '40s and '50s."

Annual events on Mountain Drive included a Scottish feast on the birthday of poet Robert Burns and a staging of Shakespeare's *Twelfth Night*. The classic Greek play *Lysistrata* was often performed in the empty swimming pool at the Hyde residence. The modern hot tub was said to have been invented on Mountain Drive as well. Joan Baez, Dylan Thomas and Lawrence Ferlinghetti were known to be familiar neighborhood guests. Michael Peake, son of famed artist Channing Peake, resided on Mountain Drive for more than 20 years and documented many of the goings-on with a keen photographic eye.

In addition to the pageants and performances, the residents also held smaller, more informal gatherings. As Chiacos recalled, "The Mountain Drive men met as the Sunset Club and once a week, every Sunday, they would gather on Jack Boegle's ocean view terrace. Here, they discussed matters of gravity as they watched the sun go down and drank wine. They sometimes shot empty dog food cans across the hills from an old homemade cannon to celebrate their masculinity."

In a retrospective story on Mountain Drive, journalist Katherine Stewart noted, "Before long, the women drummed up a gathering of their own, a knitting circle called Stitch and Bitch. And one day in 1962, Bill Neely and ceramist Ed Schertz, conspiring to wage a mock conflict, declared a Pot War. Dressed in Renaissance garb—that is, Renaissance garb as imagined by a pair of mid-20th-century bohemians—they sold their pottery by the roadside, pouring wine into every purchased ceramic cup while musicians with guitars and recorders entertained the growing crowds, and a new tradition had taken root."

Winemaking became part of the Mountain Drive lifestyle in the mid 1950s. As the story goes, resident Frank Robinson saw an advertisement announcing 20 barrels and a redwood wine vat for sale at Kinevan Ranch on San Marcos Pass between Santa Barbara and the Santa Ynez Valley. He didn't have enough money to make the purchase by himself, so Bobby Hyde pitched in, and they hauled the barrels and vat down to the Hyde property.

Another neighbor, Bill Neely, took an immediate and special interest in the endeavor. Bill Neely was a man of many nicknames and many talents. Wild Bill was the name that stuck the most. In the brief biography he wrote for Neely's published journals, contemporary Allan Shields observed that Wild Bill was "village potter, wine merchant, vintner, artist, musician, actor, writer, horseman, teacher of potter and ecology and expert rough water sailor." Neely spent his summers as a ranger and naturalist at Yosemite National Park.

According to Chiacos, "Bobby Hyde had an interest in winemaking, but it was Bill Neely's dedication to the process which made it notorious."

In the fall, they bought grapes from Kinevan Ranch, but the resulting wine was "abysmal." This experience prompted them to be a bit more scientific in their subsequent winemaking efforts. They built a wine cellar out of adobe and stone. A statue of Bacchus presided over the structure.

They named their winemaking outfit the Pagan Brothers, a playful counterpoint to the famous Christian Brothers brand. In time, the wine stompings took on a communal air, guided by a steering committee called the Wine Connoisseurs and Tasters United, whose motto was, "United we stand, united we fall."

Word began to spread as the neighborhood winemaking rituals became more and more elaborate, colorful and, well, naughty. In 1965, Hollywood came knocking, and the Mountain Drive community contracted with Paramount Pictures to film their annual wine stomp for *Seconds*, a movie starring Rock Hudson. The $5,000 earned from the deal was put into a trust to be loaned to residents in need.

By the time Bill Greenough arrived in 1968 at the age of 23, the harvest rituals were fully established. Bill was perfectly positioned to be embraced by the village elders: Bill Neely lived below him, Frank Robinson next to him, and

Jack Boegle above him. They liked the fact that Bill owned a flatbed truck that was perfect for hauling grapes.

At harvest time, 20 or so residents would hop into their trucks and drive two hours north to Paso Robles, where Neely had struck up an arrangement with a winegrower named Mel Casteel. There, in the vineyard, Casteel would have a bonfire and cook a deer over it.

"We would eat the deer and drink wine," Bill said. "Eventually, people would drift off to sleep in the vineyard or under the walnut trees."

On the day of the wine stomp, after picking and hauling the grapes back to Mountain Drive, the men would mirthfully de-stem the grapes by rubbing them over chicken wire. Their other job was to select a "Wine Queen" from among the women in the neighborhood, young and old. All sorts of unprintable debate ensued before they conducted their vote.

Meanwhile, the women would prepare a feast at Neely's home above the cellar. When the meal was ready, they would attach a note to a brick and throw the brick from the patio of the house. The brick would tumble down the slope to the cellar, signaling that lunch was now being served. They ate at a 25-foot-long table that was straight out of a Chaucer tale.

By early afternoon, the meal was over, and it was time to stomp the grapes. The new Wine Queen was always the first to disrobe and climb into the vat. She wasn't alone for long. As the revelers jumped and jostled in their birthday suits, a new vintage was born underfoot.

Bill's older brother George has only worn shoes three times in his adult life, and it's not for lack of resources. The Greenough family wasn't rich, at least not by Montecito standards. But they were well off, and money was never an issue. As far back as Bill can remember, his brother just marched to his own beat, shoeless.

George is today a living legend in surfing circles. He began riding the waves in the mid 1950s at the popular surf breaks Rincon to the south and Hollister Ranch to the north. He is credited with inventing the modern surfboard fin. Shunning the popular longboards of the day, George invented his own spoon-shaped kneeboard called the Velo in 1965, earning him fame as "the original shortboard revolutionary." According to the California Surf Museum, "George...performed surfing maneuvers that had never been seen before. He could take off deep in the pocket, come flying out to make a top turn, and then return back deep to the pocket. He was the first to perfect riding in the barrel of a wave with ease."

George later became an innovator in surf photography and cinematography, releasing two feature films in the early 1970s. Pink Floyd teamed up with George to provide music for his experimental film, *Echoes*. The classic surf film *The Endless Summer* features George in an early scene. Ironically, George was a follower of the endless winter, splitting his time between residences in Montecito and Byron Bay, Australia, which enabled him to avoid the summer crowds and enjoy the powerful winter swells without interruption. He now lives in Byron Bay full time.

To say that George's apple fell far from the family tree would be a gross understatement. The same could be said for Bill. Their father was a Harvard graduate steeped in East Coast traditions and mannerisms. He belonged to the Mayflower Society, whose members count themselves among the direct descendants of the pilgrims who established the Plymouth Colony. He was a descendant of famed American sculptor and essayist Horatio Greenough. His mother hailed from the wealthy Bliss family.

"My parents tried to put George through tennis lessons, riding lessons, things like that," Bill said. "And he just hated it. He did a lot of things to piss our father off, which wasn't hard to do, because he was so concerned with order and appearances. I remember one time, George was wearing pants without a belt. My father said, 'You need a belt, you're not properly dressed without a belt.' So George grabbed a piece of ivy, tied it around two of the belt loops, and said, 'There, I have a belt.'"

From day one, George wasn't going to toe the Greenough family line. He inexplicably tumbled out of the womb a free spirit, and that was that. "He rebelled from day one," Bill said. "He never bought into the system."

Bill, however, made an effort to fit in. Like his father, he went to boarding school and college. He belonged to the country club and dabbled in the rituals of high society. Soon, however, he found the rituals to be lacking in vigor, or even purpose. The people around him weren't really living, as much as dying in slow motion.

"I tried living that lifestyle, going out every night in a coat and tie, drinking, all that stuff," Bill said. "It was fun for a while, but it was pointless. I knew I was just wasting time. There was no end to it."

Drugs were becoming a problem with Bill's peers as well. He had a friend who died of a heroin overdose. Bill also saw people clinging to Santa Barbara like a cliff, as if leaving America's Riviera was unthinkable. "If you have to wash dishes, you wash dishes," Bill said. "Just so long as you can live in Santa Barbara...I just couldn't go on like that. No one was going anywhere."

For Bill, moving to Mountain Drive was a departure point, a pivotal shift in outlook and trajectory. He had crossed the dividing line between the establishment and the anti-establishment. It was there that he not only learned to love wine, but to truly embrace life as well. Mountain Drive expanded his horizons, and ultimately set him free.

The Mountain Drive experience alone, however, did not explain Bill's next move, the one to Saucelito Canyon.

What drove him to take on a task of such physical enormity and isolation? He could have lived on Easy Street, given his family's financial foundation. He could have remained on Mountain Drive, in the neighborhood's generous comfort zone. Instead, he moved to the canyon to conduct a one-man battle with the chaparral.

Bill himself didn't have a good explanation for it. All he could say was that he had acquired a taste for the do-it-yourself work ethic, and that he felt an inner urge to seek new challenges beyond the sunny slopes of Santa Barbara. He wanted to attempt things, to build things, and create things. He couldn't abide the thought of remaining idle.

His brother George set the early example. When George needed diving weights, he didn't buy them. He made a mold out of aluminum, and then poured molten lead into the mold to make them himself. Later, in 1970 when the local surf was becoming increasingly crowded, George started building his own yacht for his "final escape" to Australia. The yacht featured a self-made wind-powered generator.

Bill also admired the many World War II veterans who settled in Santa Barbara. Unlike the denizens of Montecito's upper crust, the veterans strutted around with a kick-ass lust for both life and work. They had won the war. They were kings of the world, at least in spirit.

The veterans could do anything, it seemed. They could fish, dive, weld, build boats and operate cranes. A couple of them started a cesspool-pumping business. They converted a few army trucks and painted them blue. Bill would see them tearing around the roads of Montecito. In time, he noticed, the number of trucks began to multiply. A prosperous little business had been created. One person's excrement, it turned out, was another's American dream.

Bill enjoyed another formative experience as a boarder at Dunn School in the Santa Ynez Valley over the mountain from Santa Barbara. Back then, the Santa Ynez Valley wasn't the upscale wine country that it is today. There were no boutiques or even vineyards. It was decades before Michael Jackson built his infamous Neverland Ranch in the valley.

Bill attended Dunn School starting in 1958, two years after it had been established on an old farm. The kids lived in converted chicken coops. Mr. Dunn was an Oxford graduate and a former major in the British army. He would not let his kids believe their school was inferior to the established private schools in Santa Barbara. His motto was: Attempt not, but achieve.

Bill joined the varsity soccer team while in the ninth

grade, as there weren't enough older boys available. Their practice field was full of rocks, and they used garbage cans as goals. The team was regularly routed by the other schools. In Bill's third year, however, they went undefeated.

"The other schools were stunned," Bill said. "That's how it was with Mr. Dunn. He had us believing that if we worked hard enough, we could do anything. Nothing was handed to us. If the juniors wanted a clubhouse where they could go smoke, they built it. The school bought the lumber, the French teacher gave them some pointers, and off they went. Attempt not, but achieve. You want a building? Go build it."

By the time he was a young man, Bill was, in some ways, leading a double life. On the exterior, he was just another son of a well-to-do Montecito family, destined to live the country club life.

But inside, a different sort of fire was burning, stoked by childhood heroes—his brother, Mr. Dunn and the brawny men who had defeated the Nazis—and ultimately set ablaze by the experiences on Mountain Drive.

"I didn't know it at the time, but I had a lot of self confidence," Bill said. "There was nothing I didn't think I could do."

Through the prism of time and sentimentality, it would be tempting to view Mountain Drive as a purely idyllic community, a place where the fun and games never ceased, and where everyone lived in bawdy harmony.

But the truth is that, despite its cultural brilliance and indelible legacy, Mountain Drive was imperfect. "Like any other American neighborhood in the '50s and '60s, alcoholism, drug abuse, divorce, childish selfishness and economic struggle took their toll," wrote Chiacos. "The Mountain Drivers' gallant effort to thwart the forces of drab conformity, venture into 'free love' alternative lifestyles, and embrace joyous hedonism, eventually succumbed to a more conservative style. Such is the way of the world. Idealism is co-opted, commercialized, or simply trampled to death."

In some ways, Mountain Drive was a victim of its own achievements. Jack Boegle complained of "the Mountain Drive myth," which "lured many a promising soul with artistic talent plus a permanent aversion to manual labor or any paid employment. They appear perennially, eat our beans and bread, drink from any open bottle, and depart gaily—lissomly leaving the sink full of dishes."

Boegle urged his neighbors to suppress the myth. That way, the "worthy few we value will find their way to Mountain Drive Village without a siren song of fantasy and be most welcome."

In 1966, the Pagan Brothers' wine cellar was vandalized,

and half of the aging vintage was stolen. In his journal, Neely wrote of his "pain and anger," and of his suspicions that the "marijuana boys" were the culprits. The boys, he wrote, had been camping on Bobby Hyde's property, and had been raided by the sheriff the week before for possessing drugs.

Neely cleaned up the cellar with a heavy heart. "Very sadly, I locked the cellar with a double lock," he wrote. "Once we were safe on Mountain Drive. Now we have to be careful, especially of the transient marijuana boys. This has discouraged us from our annual Summer Solstice celebration."

All was not idyllic for Bill on Mountain Drive, either. After living there for three years, he partnered with two friends to purchase a 12-acre mountainside lot across the street. He hired an architect and a contractor with the intent of building his dream house. The problem was that his wife was anxious to leave Santa Barbara. She had a bad relationship with her mother, and she wanted to get away. Yet here was Bill, building a house on Mountain Drive. It wasn't that Bill was averse to leaving the area. But he wanted to see the project through. The marriage began to falter.

When Bill's wife ran off with the contractor, it solved one problem, but created another. Who was going to run the subcontractors now? Bill didn't have a choice. He did it himself. He had done some construction work before, so he wasn't a novice. Still, he had a lot to learn, and he had to do it on the fly. He ended up doing a lot of the work himself.

Finishing the house took longer than expected, and by the time it was done*, Bill was spent—and already thinking about his next move, the one that would eventually lead him to Saucelito Canyon.

*In 2008, the ferocious wildfire known as the "Tea Fire" tore through Mountain Drive and destroyed many of the original homes in the neighborhood—including the one Bill had built 40 years earlier. As D.J. Palladino of the Santa Barbara Independent put it, "Fire has always loomed as the great predator in the daily life and legend of Mountain Drive. Last week it looked like fire had finally won." Left in the ruins was the smoking remnant of the "first-ever" hot tub. The late Wild Bill Neely's home, now owned by his children, was burned to the ground. Portions of the home's stone and brick walls, however, stood defiant, still decorated with Neely's pottery tiles. One of the surviving tiles was titled "Phoenix," depicting the mythic bird that rises from the ashes. Indeed, despite initial appearances, fire had not ultimately won. Order was restored, and the land would heal. The legacy of Mountain Drive lives on.

Chapter Four

RESURRECTION

BILL'S NEXT MOVE was inspired by his longtime friend Michael Benedict.

In 1971, Benedict became a winegrower, partnering with Richard Sanford to plant Sanford & Benedict Vineyard in the cool Santa Rita Hills area 40 miles northwest of Santa Barbara.

Sanford and Benedict found the climate and soil to be comparable to Burgundy, inspiring them to plant Pinot Noir. In retrospect, they were visionaries. Santa Rita Hills is today recognized as one of the world's top regions for Pinot Noir.

When Sanford and Benedict planted their vineyard, there was only one commercial winery in Santa Barbara

County. Wine grapes were not even itemized in the county's crop report until 1973, when just 200 vineyard acres were listed as bearing fruit (to put that in perspective, the county is today home to more than 20,000 vineyard acres and more than 100 wineries). The region had no track record with winegrowing. But by the early 1970s, growers and vintners like Brooks Firestone, Pierre Lafond, Richard Sanford and Michael Benedict were aiming to change that.

From a wine standpoint, Santa Barbara County was the wild west, a viticultural frontier where the settlers enjoyed no guarantee of success, and where the cost of failure would be immense. Many viewed the local winegrowers as nothing more than brazen gamblers. But in their own estimation, they were pioneers.

Bill had always enjoyed the winemaking process—and the resulting wine—on Mountain Drive. Now his friend was embarking on a grand adventure to actually plant and farm a vineyard. Bill tagged along as Benedict went looking for vineyard property, and he watched as the first vines were planted. Bill found the process fascinating, and soon he, too, was smitten with the idea of owning a vineyard.

For Bill, winegrowing signified many things. It was a good excuse to finally leave the balmy cocoon of Santa Barbara proper. It was a salve on the wound of a failed marriage. And it was yet another opportunity to achieve, not attempt.

So off he went, seeking his own little piece of viticultural earth. First, he traveled up to Paso Robles, where he had been several times to help pick grapes for the Pagan Brothers' bottlings. He looked at a handful of properties, but couldn't find the right match.

Michael Benedict was a proponent of cool-climate wine-growing, and he was in Bill's ear, evangelizing about the virtues of the "transverse" coastal valleys that opened up to the Pacific Ocean in Santa Barbara County and southern San Luis Obispo County. Whereas most California valleys paralleled the coastline, the transverse valleys—a quirk of geological evolution—ran west to east. In these valleys, the marine air met no resistance as it billowed inland. They were like funnels, sucking in the cool breath of the Pacific.

One day, Bill's realtor called. There was a property for sale in the upper Arroyo Grande Valley in southern San Luis Obispo County, about 40 miles south of the city of Paso Robles and 15 miles north of the Santa Barbara County line. The property was the old Rancho Saucelito. The granddaughters of Henry Ditmas, the original homesteader, had recently put it up for sale.

Apparently, there had been a vineyard out there, once upon a time, but the property was now essentially abandoned.

It didn't sound that great to Bill, but he figured it couldn't hurt to look. After all, the Arroyo Grande Valley was one of those rare transverse valleys that Michael Benedict was always talking about. So on a bright spring afternoon in 1974, Bill and his realtor took the long drive out to Saucelito Canyon. Bill's hopes for a successful outcome waned with each passing mile. Where was this place?

Finally, they reached the gate and drove into the heart of the property. Bill stepped out of the car. The first thing he noticed was the smell—a dusty, dry herb aroma blowing off the chaparral. Before him was an expanse of scrub and poison oak riddled with the overgrown knobs of what looked like dead vines. To the left, a tall mesa loomed like the Great Wall. To the right and behind, the wilderness ascended, cradling the old rancho. And straight ahead was the breathtaking edifice of Hi Mountain.

A cool breeze rattled through the oak trees, but that wasn't what sent the shiver up Bill's spine. It was something else, a sudden sense of feeling at home in this strange, rugged land.

$$\varsigma\heartsuit\heartsuit)$$

After escrow closed on the rancho, Bill fenced out the cattle and deer that had been grazing on the vines for so many years. He then cleared out the brush. He estimated that the original vineyard had spanned eight acres, which would have kept Henry Ditmas and his horse very busy. Of those eight acres, only five still had vines on them. Of those five vineyard acres, two were dead and beyond hope. That left three acres of struggling old Zinfandel vines that Bill was determined to resurrect.

With the animals fenced out and the brush cleared, the vines responded immediately with fresh vigorous growth. Then, on a clear, brisk morning in late September of 1974, Bill took a pick and shovel to the first vine on the south-west corner of the vineyard. He dug a three-foot diameter hole around the trunk of the vine until he reached a depth of one and a half feet, which gave him access to the bottom of the vine. He cut off all of the weaker shoots, and left the strongest of them all. While the morning was still cool, he mopped his brow as he surveyed the remainder of his task. Only 1,199 more vines to go.

During the following summer, Bill embarked on a similar task, driving 1,200 grape stakes next to each vine. The new shoots he had selected for each vine were now much longer and thicker. Each shoot was tied to a stake to form the beginning of a new head-trained vine. Now, a full 95 years after they had been planted, the old vines were poised to once again yield the gift of wine.

⌒∞⌒

By the fall of 1980, Bill had grown his first commercial crop, with six tons of fruit hanging on the three acres of old vines. It hadn't yet occurred to him to make wine. He thought of himself as a winegrower, not a winemaker. He hadn't restored the old vines because he thought they would produce anything particularly special, or because they might prove to be a favorable marketing tool. It had just seemed like the right thing to do. Why rip out a vineyard when you can reclaim it instead?

He negotiated a contract with a Paso Robles winery to buy all of the fruit for $500 per ton. He rounded up a group of friends to help pick the grapes. The grapes were picked into 40-pound lug boxes. Bill's friends bailed before it was time to stack the lug boxes onto the back of a rented flatbed truck, so Bill did it himself. The next morning, he headed out for the 40-mile trek to Paso Robles. Soon, however, the truck started lurching and finally broke down at the corner of Hi Mountain Road and Lopez Drive, just three miles from the vineyard.

As fate would have it, Bill's ex-wife's one-legged boyfriend happened to be driving by on his way into town, and Bill flagged him down. He helped Bill move the lug boxes to another rental truck that eventually showed up, but Bill had to do most of the heavy lifting, for obvious reasons. Exhausted, he got back on the road.

"I finally get to the winery in Paso," Bill said. "By then, it's three in the afternoon, it's really hot. And the owner says to me, 'Okay, just pull over next to the stemmer-crusher and start dumping them in.' And I say, 'Don't you have

anyone to help me?'" And he says, 'No, just get started.'"
I'm thinking, 'You mean I've got to handle all of these lug
boxes again?' That was selling fruit, that's what it was like."

Bill watched as the winery then made a "centennial bottling" out of grapes from his vineyard—a 1980 vintage wine
made from vines planted in 1880. "They sold it for $25 a
bottle, which was big, big money for Zinfandel in those
days," Bill said. "This was from grapes that I had grown all
year, picked by hand and moved three times in 40-pound
lug boxes. I was in the wrong business. There was just more
money in making wine than selling fruit."

More important, the wine made from his grapes was
surprisingly good. Bill saw the potential to not only make
wine, but to possibly make great wine.

The year 1980 was momentous for another reason, as
that's when Bill married Nancy. They had met 15 years
earlier in Montecito, and for Bill it was "love at first sight."
There was only one problem: they were both dating their
first spouses at the time. But they had mutual friends, and
they would occasionally cross paths over the years, and
Bill's feelings for her remained strong.

One evening in the late 1970s, Bill had an epiphany
while sipping his third martini at his outdoor camp next to
the half-built cottage overlooking the vineyard. He thought,
"I can either do what I'm doing alone and be satisfied, or
this is too beautiful and I have to share it, and my life, with

somebody." Nancy immediately came to mind. He asked her out on a date, and this time fate would not be denied. Nancy's daughter Bianca later gained two siblings—Margaret born in 1981, and Tom a few years later.

By the fall of 1982, Bill and Nancy had built a small winery facility and acquired a bond that allowed them to produce commercial wine. They still only had enough fruit to produce around 500 cases, but it was a start. Half of the crop was used to make a White Zinfandel, a blush-style wine that was fashionable at the time. The rest was used to make a red Zinfandel.

The White Zinfandel was released early the next year, and the Zinfandel Estate was bottled the following summer. Every bottle was filled and corked by hand with the help of friends. Now it was time to sell the wine.

Bill drove up and down the coast with cases of wine in the trunk of his car, stopping at restaurants and wine shops to give them a taste of his Zinfandel. The wine was met with more praise than he ever could have hoped. He eventually found his way to Santa Barbara. "I got up the nerve to visit the best, snobbiest wine shop in town," Bill said. "I walked in there with my bottle of Zinfandel and said, 'This is my wine, made from a 100-year-old vineyard. I just made it! I'd like you to try it and let me know what you think.' He was a nice guy. He tried it and said, 'That's really good. I'll take five cases.' That's when I knew we were on our way."

In the years ahead, Bill and Nancy would plant additional blocks of Zinfandel adjacent to the old vines, as well as a small block of Cabernet Sauvignon, ultimately reaching a total of 10 vineyard acres. The average production grew to 2,500 cases annually. Equipment was cobbled together as needed. One tank was inherited from a dairy operation. Used barrels were acquired from whiskey producers.

By the 1995 harvest season, all 10 acres were producing a healthy crop. Newer barrels and tanks had been incorporated into the operation. Sales were strong. Twenty-one years had passed since Bill first marched into the raggedy old vineyard with his pick and shovel. And now another crush was bearing down on him.

Henry Ditmas, the original homesteader of Rancho Saucelito,
who planted the vineyard in 1880.

The vineyard at Rancho Saucelito in 1894, with the vines spaced for farming by horse and plow, and the vertical face of Hi Mountain in the distance.

Workers with wine barrels, a small crusher and a wagon full of grape picking bins circa 1890s at neighboring St. Remy winery, which used fruit from Rancho Saucelito.

Cecil, Margaret and Barbara Ditmas, the grandchildren of Henry and Rosa Ditmas, in the vineyard at Saucelito Canyon in 1915. Bill Greenough acquired the property from Margaret and Barbara in 1974.

*Pioneering Mountain Drive vintner Bill Neely, with wife
Barbara and sons Severin and Dana, harvesting wine grapes in
Paso Robles in 1958. Photo courtesy of the Neely family.*

Clothing wasn't optional during the communal grape stompings on Mountain Drive in the 1960s–it was forbidden. Photo courtesy of Michael Peake.

Bill Greenough's older brother, famed surfer George Greenough (foreground), set an early entrepreneurial example for Bill.

When Bill arrived at Rancho Saucelito in 1974, the abandoned vineyard was just a grid of decrepit stumps ensnared in dry brush.

Bill dug into the root zones and selected the strongest shoots to retrain and reinvigorate the old vines.

By 1976, the old vines were on the path to revival, and would later produce some of California's most notable Zinfandel.

By the early 1980s, Bill had built a small winery to produce wines from Saucelito Canyon Vineyard.

The vineyard and canyon during the 1995 harvest season, with Hi Mountain on the horizon and the mesa on the left.

*The inimitable Peter shoveling grape skins from the
fermentation tank.*

The author (in hat), Adam and Peter's dog with the infamous shrink-wrapped press.

The final howl of the mysterious dead coyote.

Chapter Five

VAGABONDS

ON MY SECOND day back in the canyon, Bill handed me a 12-gauge shotgun. He gave me a quick lesson on how to use it, and taught me how to reload the shells in the shop. Then he sent me out in the vineyard to wage war against the starlings, the winged vermin that would destroy the 1995 crop if left unchecked.

History tells us that the European Starling was purposefully introduced to North America in 1890 by an academic who thought that all types of birds mentioned in William Shakespeare's plays should be released across the pond, starting in New York's Central Park. The original 60 starlings released in Central Park ultimately grew into an international nuisance of 150 million birds stretching from southern Canada to Mexico.

In other words, some pretentious assclown had started this problem, and now a hundred years later it was our problem. The local starlings would arrive in ravenous flocks, ever ready to descend en masse and peck at the fruit. Saucelito Canyon consisted of 10 precious acres of vines, and all of the wine came from this one vineyard. Every grape counted.

Therefore, bird control was an ongoing and multifaceted effort in the canyon. You started with reflective tinsel tied to the vines and endposts. The tinsel would flutter in the breeze and startle the starlings, scaring them away. But these birds were savvy creatures, and it wasn't long before they began to call the tinsel's bluff.

Propane-powered noise cannons were the second line of defense. Propane would slowly fill a bladder until it reached a tipping point, triggering a loud boom that would scare the birds out of the vineyard. In time, however, the birds would triangulate the location and timing of the cannons, ultimately determining that they were harmless noisemakers.

At some point, you needed to resort to the unpredictability of a shotgun. By the time I arrived on the property, this third line of defense was already in need of deployment.

The harvest was still several weeks off, and so bird control would become one of my routine pre-crush responsibilities. I drove into the heart of the vineyard on the Mule, the winery's ATV, and waited. Initially, the starlings steered clear of me. They would swarm over the ridge, blackening the sky in a rigid triangle like a stealth bird bomber. But at the last moment, they would scatter and retreat as I squeezed off a few impotent shots.

I needed to ratchet up the unpredictability factor, so I hopped off the Mule and hid under cover of the bushy old vines. There I waited, the August sun beating down on my neck, the vine leaves tickling my ears. About five minutes later, the black armada returned. This time, it didn't pull back. It flew right over me. I unloaded several shells, and this time the flock's retreat wasn't so orderly. Message delivered. After a few days of this, their persistence was weakened.

The canyon was otherwise quiet during that first week, but I found enough to keep me busy. Toward the end of the month, I was tasked with racking the previous 1994 vintage out of the barrels. The winery's 100 or so barrels were stacked in pairs on metal racks. The job entailed forklifting the racks down to the center of the cellar floor, then gently pumping the wine out of each barrel and into holding tanks. After the barrels were empty, they had to be wrangled off the rack, rolled along the floor and onto a barrel washer out back.

Once the barrels were empty, Bill and I filtered the wine in preparation for bottling. Bill had one small filter machine. We would load the machine with filtration pads and pump the wine through them from one tank to another.

The pads would filter out any remaining particulates in order to clarify and stabilize the wine. The process was painfully slow. As the pads began to clog up, the flow rate would slow down. But changing the pads was a chore, so you needed to get the most out of them.

In theory, I could have just left the winery periodically while the filter and pump were doing their thing. I could have gone up to the cottage for dinner, or driven the Mule up to the ridge to watch the sunset. But filtration is like babysitting. Everything's great until you turn your back and find the toddler dangling from the fire escape. Sure enough, one time while I was out back washing a tank, the hose blew off the filter intake. The pads must have clogged up, and the weakest link in the chain had blown. Thankfully, I caught it quickly, but not before a few gallons of fine Zinfandel were flushed down the cellar drain.

I spent several nights keeping an eye on the filter as we pushed to meet the bottling date. Each filtration shift would finally end with me standing in clouds of steam, washing out the last emptied tank.

The mobile bottling truck rolled in at the crack of dawn on August 31. Bill's wife Nancy and their kids, Tom and Margaret, arrived to pitch in. Bottling was a festive respite from the solitary days of filtration.

The mobile bottling line was crammed into a small semi-trailer. Inside, the empty bottles were dumped onto a conveyer. As the bottles circled around the inside of the trailer, they were sparged, filled, corked, foiled and labeled. The mobile bottling crew would then insert the finished bottles into case boxes. Our job was to catch the heavy boxes as they rolled down the conveyer and stack them on pallets in a very specific configuration. Once the pallet was full, we would encircle it with shrink wrap, then forklift it onto an awaiting truck.

It took a few days to finish bottling. The barrels and tanks were all empty now. The decks were clear, and the table was officially set for harvest. The canyon quieted down again. Now it was time to get the crush equipment in order. In the days ahead, I pressure-washed the crusher, scrubbed the picking bins and cleaned the sorting conveyer.

Bill seemed happy to have someone there full time, someone to whom he could delegate these lonely tasks. I never did figure out what was different that year, why he'd felt compelled to call me out of the blue and recruit me back to the canyon. I suspected that he just needed a bit of a break, physical and mental. He was still deeply involved, but he could now get away when he needed to.

Meanwhile, I was adapting to the isolation of the canyon and the novelty of living in the rustic cottage. For now, all was calm, the days rhythmic in their routines. It was still early in the season. Yet for me, much had already changed.

"Hey, wha's up?"

One late afternoon, while I was walking out of the vine-yard after a round of bird control, a guy named Peter came barreling down the driveway and screeched to a halt in his pockmarked white Toyota mini truck. I'd never met Peter, but his reputation preceded him.

Those were his first words to me: "Hey, wha's up?" And they were the first words I would hear on many a morning for the next two months.

"Not much," I said.

"You Christopher?" he said. Apparently, he'd heard of me, too.

Peter, I'd been told, had only worked the previous two harvests, but he was already a Saucelito Canyon legend. He was the guy who'd once knocked himself out while driving fence posts. He was a notorious menace on the forklift, as evidenced by the splintered ceiling beams in the winery cellar.

Among his many extracurricular pursuits, Peter was a part-time bartender by night, which contributed to his frequent tardiness. And then there were his tales of frisky young women who allegedly kept him busy at night. It was hard to sort out fact from fiction, but as the harvest wore on, he started to look less like Pinocchio and more like Casanova as more than one cute girl came out to the winery to bring him lunch. He must have been doing something right to get these girls to drive all the way out to the canyon with sandwiches.

One of them looked suspiciously young. Bill asked Peter, "Do you know how old she is?"

Peter thought about it for a second, and replied, "No."

Bill said, "Well, you might want to find out."

Peter, I would soon learn, was reliable in an unreliable sort of way, meaning that, yes, he would sometimes show up late, and sometimes fail to show up at all, but he genuinely regretted his unreliability and made up for it by busting his butt when he did show up. Most people, when calling in sick, would say something about the flu or a sprained ankle. Peter, however, would call in sick with such exotic maladies as "the terminal shits."

Now here was the legend himself, and this was my first look at him. He wore his sandy blond hair long, in a ponytail. On his face, he wore a perpetual Cheshire Cat grin. I liked that grin.

"Lone Star?" I asked.

Lone Star, I'd decided, was the mascot beer of the 1995 harvest, if only because I could buy a case of it at Long's Drugs for $10 during the infrequent journeys into town. Plus, Bill hated Texas for some reason, which made it funny to have around.

"Sure," Peter said. "My dad, he drinks Pabst. It ain't too bad, either."

"Why pay four bucks for a sixer of Bud?"

"Exactly."

We sipped our cold ones. I learned that Peter lived in nearby Lopez Canyon, which is probably why he seemed at ease out here in the boondocks. The evening sun simmered above the mesa, and a pack of starlings arced around a distant knoll. Peter leaned on the bed of his truck and asked, "So, what you been doing?"

I could tell he was curious. As far as I was concerned, I was an old hand at Saucelito Canyon. But to Peter, I was the new kid on the block.

"Bird control. Filtration. Building a bin dumper."

"Good deal," he said. "You need help with that dumper?"

"Not sure. So far, so good, I think."

"Well, let me know. I've got the time. We could bang it out. Give me a call."

"I just might," I said, knowing that I wouldn't. I was having a hard enough time keeping myself busy without resorting to things like scrubbing the cellar floors or whacking weeds. The grapes were ripening slowly, and the first pick was still a ways off.

"Give me a hand?" he asked, nodding to the back of his truck, where there was a large yard mower. He explained that he'd borrowed it from Bill and was returning it. We set our beers down and eased the mower to the ground.

"See you for harvest?" I said.

"For sure."

Peter finished his beer and tore off in a cloud of dust. I already knew at that point that we'd get along. I sensed that he was a guy who could take the worst tasks in stride and see the humor in them. In other words, he was built to work the crush.

⌒𖣘)

For most of the year, Bill flew solo, working the land and tending to his barrels amid the quietude of the winter, spring and summer seasons. He would hire help for pruning and some of the other big jobs. But on the average day in February or June, it was just Bill out there, toiling away.

Come the crunch time of autumn, however, he had to reckon with 10 acres of vines bursting with 30 or more tons of fruit that needed to be handmade into 2,500 cases of wine.

To handle the harvest load, Bill needed help. But he never mounted much of a recruitment effort. He seemed to prefer the randomness of friends of friends, word of mouth, university job boards and chance encounters. Inevitably, the warm bodies would come, somehow, from somewhere.

Enter the 1995 Saucelito Canyon harvest crew: Peter, the jester; Richard, the engineer; Adam, the drummer; Clarence, the shy guy; Luis and his team of pickers; and myself.

Richard was the academic yin to Peter's hard-partying yang. He was Bill's age, and he was an aerospace engineer. Richard didn't need the harvest wages, but he loved wine and liked the excitement of the crush. We'd crossed paths a few times when I'd worked the harvest there three years earlier. He was a talented fix-it man, and when the winery's rickety electrical system went on the blink—as it often did—Richard would find a way to power us back up.

Richard had been working with Bill since the late 1980s, and he could tell stories that made our hardships sound like amenities. He remembered when there was no forklift or sorting conveyor in the canyon. During harvest, he and Bill would have to pitchfork the grapes straight from the field bin and into the crusher. They would then dart their hands in and out to remove bad clusters while trying not to lose their digits by getting them caught in the crusher's steel auger. He remembered standing in the back of Bill's white Isuzu pickup truck in 105-degree heat, trimming the overgrown vines with a gas-powered hedger as Bill slowly drove backward through the vine rows while complaining about the truck's lack of air conditioning.

Adam was a quiet guy who looked like Kirk Hammett, the guitarist for Metallica. He had called after seeing the job posted somewhere. He had an olive complexion, a skinny frame and long, frizzy black hair. His passion was playing the drums. He was agreeable and always happy to laugh along with us, but he rarely initiated the laughs himself. This was just a job to him, like landscaping or construction. He was an artist, and his calling was music, not wine.

Clarence would arrive some weeks after harvest started. He was referred by a friend of a friend of Nancy. Clarence's family owned a local sporting goods store. He was an un-failingly genuine young man with a gee-whiz quality that seemed straight out of a bygone era. Having never worked in a winery, he was a bit tentative at the start. But he proved to be a capable asset, and in time he revealed a sly wit that lurked beneath his polite exterior. We called him the win-ery's assassin-for-hire.

Luis ran the picking crew. He was an older man with a thick mustache and an aristocratic visage. He ran his crew with friendly authority. His English was pretty good, but he and Bill occasionally ran into a language barrier, no doubt exacerbated by Bill's tendency to mumble his words. This is how, at one point during the harvest, the crew starting pick-ing Cabernet Sauvignon fruit and dumping it into a bin full of Zinfandel. Thankfully, the error was caught early.

This was the year of *El Chupacabra*, the so-called "goat sucker" alien-vampire hybrid that was allegedly terrorizing Latin America, killing livestock and stealing babies.

El Chupacabra was the new celebrity of the conspiracy crowd, and even some mainstream media outlets were re-porting on the growing fear of this mysterious predator, with recent sightings in Mexico and the Southwest. Naturally, it became a point of discussion and bonding with Luis. Much of his crew had recently traveled from south of the border. What did they know? What were they hearing?

As for Bill, it wasn't the goat suckers that were keeping him up at night. The vineyard had a problem. The fruit wasn't ripening, it was stuck in neutral.

Chapter Six

RELUCTANT VINES

ON THE MORNING of September 12, I trudged into the vineyard to grab grape samples from each Zinfandel block, picking a grape here and a grape there. I placed the grapes in Ziploc bags, one marked for each block.

After I'd walked the entire vineyard, I returned to the lab. I mashed up the grapes within each baggy, then dabbed the juice onto a small device called a refractometer, which gave me the Brix readings for each vineyard block. Brix is the term for sugar level in an aqueous solution. In winemaking, it's used as a measurement of fruit ripeness.

Bill kept a three-ring calendar on the lab counter. I dutifully recorded the Brix readings, then flipped the page back to the previous week for comparison. I was stunned—

the sugar levels should have been gaining, but instead they were stalled, virtually unmoved from a week earlier and hanging back in the underripe range of 16.7 to 19.2 Brix. In fact, despite steady temperatures in the eighties, the Brix readings had actually regressed a bit in some blocks.

So at the very time that the vineyard should have been going forward, it was going nowhere, and in some spots, backwards.

Bill rolled into the canyon later that morning, and I showed him the readings I'd recorded in the calendar. He looked them over for a second, then flipped the page back to the previous week, and said, "What the heck?"

I just shrugged my shoulders.

"You sure you're randomizing things out there?" Bill said. "You have to almost act like you're blind when you're pulling those grapes."

He was reminding me that it's easy to have a subconscious bias. If you weren't careful, you might find yourself gravitating toward picking grapes from the top of the clusters, or the bottom of the clusters. Or you might have a tendency to select grapes with a riper color, or a less ripe color. If you did that, then you would skew the results away from the true average. Zinfandel was known as an uneven ripener, so randomizing it was especially crucial.

"Yeah, I'm really trying," I said. "I squint my eyes when I approach the vines, and I turn my head away from the clusters when I reach for the grapes. I'm not even looking at them when I pick 'em. It's as random as I can get."

"Okay, well, how about we try it again this afternoon?"

"Will do," I said.

This was my first indication that he was concerned about the state of the vineyard. Why else would he want to run Brix samples twice in one day with the harvest still a ways off? He was having a hard time believing the readings, and he wanted verification.

At 3:30 p.m., I returned to the vineyard. The temperature was now 90 degrees, and my legs were getting fatigued from walking up and down the soft dirt of the vine rows. I returned to the lab and ran the numbers. They were nearly identical to what I'd recorded that morning.

There was no explanation in the natural world for what was happening. The grapes were simply not ripening. They were stuck on the precipice of harvest, refusing to go over the cliff. If something didn't change soon, the grapes would be in a shambles, and the 1995 vintage would be a bitter mess.

～⌒～

On September 15, Bill had me run morning and afternoon samples again. There was some slight improvement in the readings, but by September 22 the numbers hadn't nudged much, and a few of the blocks were still stuck in the range of 18 to19 degrees Brix.

The weather had been perfect for ripening. Cool conditions will slow the pace of ripening. Conversely, if it gets hot to the tune of 95 degrees or more, the grapes will temporarily shut down. But we were getting steady warm temperatures in the 70s and 80s.

A level of 24 degrees Brix in the grapes will roughly equate to a wine of 13.5 percent alcohol, while a level of 26 degrees Brix will roughly equate to a wine of 15 percent alcohol. This is because during fermentation, the yeasts convert the sugar into alcohol and carbon dioxide gas. The more sugar there is to convert, the higher the alcohol becomes.

Bill tended to pick on the lower end of the Brix scale. He didn't want high alcohols and ultra-ripe flavors in his wines. He wanted to make a wine that had restraint and balance and a sense of place. In terms of ripeness, he wasn't asking a lot of his grapes, and yet they were still refusing to cooperate. He needed them to at least get close to 24 degrees Brix.

Sugar level wasn't the only consideration when determining when to pick grapes. Bill also paid attention to phenolic, or physiological, ripeness, which focuses more on texture, flavor and tannin maturity. But sugar was still the tail that wagged the harvest dog. If your sugar was too low or too high, it could be hard to overcome.

By the morning of September 28, all of the blocks remained stuck in the range of 19 to 21 degrees Brix. By comparison, during the preceding 1994 and 1993 harvests, the entire Zinfandel crop had been picked by the end of September despite significantly cooler autumn weather.

Things were going sideways in the canyon. I could tell Bill was wondering if there was something wrong not just in a momentary sense, but in a macro sense. He'd seen everything out here, but he hadn't seen this.

Zinfandel is a thin-skinned grape, and the clusters are tightly packed. This makes it prone to bunch rot, particularly if conditions are moist or wet. Some level of rot was unavoidable even under normal conditions. The key was to keep it in check.

The problem was, the later in the season we got, the more exposed we were to a possible cold front or rainfall that could send the rot into overdrive. Fall rain was unusual, but it happened. No winemaker wants to choose between picking underripe fruit or rotting grapes.

Thankfully, for now, the weather was holding, but Bill kept a close eye on the forecast as we tumbled toward October with all of the grapes still hanging out on the vines.

The other concern was that the vines might just shut down before reaching the finish line. When vines shut down, they stop putting energy into ripening fruit and start heading into hibernation mode for the winter.

The vineyard was dry farmed, meaning that there was no irrigation. There'd been a couple of big storms early in the year, but water and soil moisture were always a concern when dry farming. The vines needed to be sufficiently hydrated to get through the harvest season without shutting down early.

If the vines shut down, the fruit would begin to dehydrate. The sugar level would suddenly soar, and Bill would be forced to pick the grapes whether he liked it or not. It would be a fake ripeness born of dehydration, and the resulting wine would likely be flabby and unbalanced.

After I showed Bill the readings on September 28, he moved his finger down the calendar page and jabbed it at the date of October 1, as if it held some sort of special significance.

"The crush is going to be a circus this year," he said.

I'd already figured that. Because the grapes were taking so long to ripen, our window for picking and processing them was getting shorter by the day. The harvest would be compressed, and a compressed harvest was a recipe for chaos. It was like telling a chef he needed to prepare the usual amount of dinners, but in half the time.

For now, however, there was no need to borrow trouble. Bill left early for home, leaving me to my janitorial tasks.

That evening, I sat on the cabin porch, enjoying a cold Lone Star, watching the twilight fade behind Hi Mountain. Bill and Nancy had left the cottage many years earlier, after they had children. It would have been impractical to raise infants out there, so they'd moved closer to town.

Like the winery, the cottage was powered by the diesel generator. I knew that Bill viewed post-work electricity as a luxury, not a necessity. He was the one who replenished the diesel tank, so he would know if I was luxuriating.

So after dinner, as usual, I shut the generator off and read a book on the couch in the glow of an oil lamp. At some point, I nodded off. The coyotes woke me up sometime past midnight, and I stumbled through the dark until I found my bed.

⌒⁰⁰⌒

Living in the cottage at Saucelito Canyon was a glorified form of camping. The doors had no locks. They consisted of wood frames around full-length panels of glass. On one of my first nights staying out there, I about jumped out of my shoes when I was walking down the hallway and, out of the corner of my eye, saw something moving right next to me. It was a coyote peering through the glass door. We seemed to startle each other. It scampered away as my heart pounded against my ribs.

Sometimes it was hard to fall asleep with all the things that went bump in the night. The old wood planks of the porch would creak under the weight of lurking animals. Sometimes, it would sound just like a person walking. Creatures would also amble along the roof, often dislodging acorns that would rattle on their way down the shingles before clanging onto the porch. Owls would hoot, and raccoons would scratch and, in the distance, the coyotes would start howling.

What made me even jumpier than animals on the roof at night was the rare sound of a truck or car coming down the dirt road just beyond the gate to the property. The road led to other ranches and cabins, but it wasn't a frequented route. Very few vehicles went past the winery during the day, and even fewer traveled the road during the evening. So the sound of a car at 2 a.m. was always a bit unnerving.

Vandalism and theft were a concern. With a pair of bolt cutters, anyone could get through the gate and into the winery and do some real damage. A lot of people had worked for Bill over the years. A lot of people knew what was out there. It only took one. Whenever I was awakened by the sound of a vehicle, it was hard not to sleep with one eye open for the rest of the night.

In time, I adapted to the isolation, and learned which sounds to ignore. For the first few weeks, I was itching to get into town, to go to a grocery or convenience store or restaurant, just out of pure habit. But those urges soon waned, and even when I found myself with a free afternoon or evening, I was more often than not content to just stay cozy in the canyon. My biorhythms were being rewired.

As we lurched into the first day of October without a single grape picked, I noticed something different in the air, a charged stillness, and a sudden slant to the light. It was the unmistakable first kiss of autumn.

I sensed that the grapes would notice the change in air and light, too, and that they would now start to make up for lost time. I suspected that the pin would soon be pulled from the proverbial harvest grenade. It couldn't come fast enough.

For the moment, however, it was business as usual. I hopped on the Mule to prowl for deer and starlings. The deer loved to eat the fruit, but they were easy to chase out of the vineyard. Once they heard the Mule coming, they would bounce elegantly out of the vines and over the ineffective deer fence.

The sun grew mean by late morning. By afternoon, the temperature would reach 89 degrees. It was proving to be a classic "Indian summer" along the coast. In many parts of the country, temperatures were sinking. Here, however, they were only warming up. This was the time of year when California often went up in smoke.

As I looped back around the perimeter of the vineyard, I saw something odd out of the corner of my eye. I turned around for a closer look and saw that it was a dead coyote, in full rigor mortis with its mouth open in a silent howl.

How could a coyote just drop dead like that out in the

open? If it was injured or perishing of old age, wouldn't it have skulked off to some hiding place? Yet if it had been preyed upon and killed, why was it so intact? There were bears and other predators in the canyon. But what kind of creature would catch and strike a coyote dead, then just leave it there, unscathed? Could it be a chupacabra? Nah... But if not that, then what?

When Bill arrived later, I showed him the coyote. He was puzzled, too. This was another thing he hadn't seen before. We just left it there. There were more important matters at hand than trying to dispose of a wild animal carcass.

As it turned out, however, it wasn't the last we would hear from that dead little desert dog.

Chapter Seven

GAME ON

THE SUN CONTINUED to sizzle. On October 2, the mercury reached 95 degrees. Two days later, it topped out at 93 degrees. By the end of the week, it began to cool down, but not before the grapes had gotten a much-needed kick in the pants. The hotter weather was just what they'd been waiting for, and they'd responded with accelerated ripening. Dehydration remained in check, and the grapes were in pretty good shape. Mother Nature had swooped in and saved the day.

The vineyard was farmed as five separate blocks: Old Block (3 acres); Willow Block (1.5 acres), Winery Block (2.5 acres); House Block (2 acres); and Bordeaux Triangle (1 acre). All of the blocks were planted to Zinfandel vines, except for the Bordeaux Triangle, which was home to a small assortment of Bordeaux varieties.

I continued to run grape samples, and the numbers were starting to look promising. On October 4, the upper Old Block clocked in at 23 degrees Brix, with the lower Old Block right behind at 22.9 degrees Brix. The House and Willow blocks were right there as well, and the Winery block was trailing at 20.5 degrees Brix.

The pace of our preparation work began to accelerate. The languid days of waiting were about to end, and we were energized by the thought of it. Bill showed up pulling an old Prowler camping trailer that I'd never seen before. He parked it in the dirt turnabout in front of the winery. I didn't ask, but it looked like he planned to move some of his administrative work out of the cramped lab and into the slightly more spacious Prowler. I suspected that he also liked the idea of having a place where he could get away from the rest of us if he wanted to, if only for a few minutes.

By October 6, the crush was finally on. After so many weeks of waiting, head scratching and nail biting, Bill had determined that the time had come to start picking the Old Block. Luis and his crew arrived at the crack of dawn and started picking. I hustled down to the winery. Bill showed up shortly thereafter, followed by Peter, Richard and Adam. We scrambled to set up all of the equipment before Luis hauled the first bin of grapes out of the vineyard.

There was a buzz in the air, but Bill was quiet. There would be no rah-rah speeches from Bill. He seemed tight and clenched. He was like a quarterback before a big game, focused and confident, but not immune to a few butterflies in the gut. Bill needed the crush to go well. Here in the canyon, you only got so many grapes and so many chances to make a good wine each year, and it all started right now.

The Old Block was right next to the winery, and we could hear the pickers chattering as they cut the clusters from the vines and dropped them into small plastic bins. The pickers dumped the contents of their individual bins into a large half-ton bin that was forked onto the back of the tractor. In time, that larger bin was full, and Luis drove it out of the vineyard and deposited it in the dirt area in front of the winery. The fruit looked gorgeous—deep purple Zinfandel grapes and bright green stems glistening with morning dew.

"I got this," Peter said, jumping on the forklift. He sped over to the bin, picked it up and drove over to the wooden bin dumper that we had positioned on the concrete pad in front of the winery.

I had built the bin dumper out of two-by-fours and plywood, based on one that Richard had created a few years earlier. It took me several days and taxed my meager construction skills, and now I wondered if it would hold up.

The bin dumper was emblematic of the "Saucelito Way,"

a one-off invention born of necessity, and not to be found anywhere else. It was designed to carefully transition the grapes from the big vineyard bin and onto the green conveyer belt that Bill used for fruit sorting.

The main part of the dumper was like a tall table, with four legs supporting a flat expanse of plywood about five feet off the ground. Above the far end of the plywood was a retaining bar, and beneath the retaining bar was another piece of plywood slanting downward like a chute.

Peter lifted the bin and gently placed it onto the plywood table. Then he backed out until the forks were just touching the back edge of the bin. He lifted the forks and the bin began to tip, and fruit started tumbling down the chute.

When the bin reached an angle of around 45 degrees, Peter jumped off the forklift, grabbed a garden rake and started gently feeding more clusters down the chute and onto the conveyor. The rest of us stood on either side of the conveyor and started sorting. Once we cleared the chute, Peter returned to the forklift and tipped the bin ever further. We repeated the process until Peter could tip the bin completely over and into the retaining bar, spilling the last of the bin's contents onto the chute. The first bin of the 1995 harvest was now clear.

Bill didn't pay his pickers by the ton, but rather by the hour. This incentivized the pickers to take their time and leave any compromised fruit behind. Nevertheless, questionable stuff still found its way into the picking bins.

Therefore, Bill insisted on carefully sorting the fruit before it went into the crusher-destemmer, as it gave us one last chance to discard any unripe or moldy clusters, as well as errant leaves or other debris. He didn't want anything impure to make it into the fermentation mix. Fruit sorting would later become standard operating procedure in modern winemaking, but at the time Bill was ahead of the curve.

The sorting conveyer was angled upward, and the good fruit was allowed to tumble off the far end and into the crusher-destemmer. The crusher-destemmer consisted of a rectangular funnel that directed the clusters down into a whirling stainless steel cylinder pocked with small evenly spaced holes. As the clusters tumbled around the cylinder, the grapes were jostled loose from the stems, falling through the holes of the cylinder and into a reserve area below. Bill called his crusher-destemmer "the Cuisinart," as it made a loud whine and beat the hell out of the grapes. He had plans to invest in a bigger and better machine, but for now we were stuck with the Cuisinart.

From the Cuisinart's reserve area, the grapes—now destemmed and slightly crushed—were pumped out through a hose that ran through the winery's back doorway and into an awaiting fermentation vessel. The stems, meanwhile, would tumble out of the back of the cylinder and into a waste bin.

Thus, in the span of about 50 feet, from the front of the winery to the back, the grape clusters were transformed from their native state into carefully sorted fermentation fodder.

Once the first fermentation vessel was full that morning, Bill stepped out of the lab carrying a plastic pitcher filled with a mixture of warm water and commercial winemaking yeast. He stood over the side of the fermentation bin and poured it in, the opaque liquid splashing over the grape skins. Peter climbed atop the side of the bin and mashed the juicy grape mass with a long wooden paddle to spread the yeast out.

This moment signified the initial flashpoint of fermentation as the yeast began to consume the grape sugar and turn it into alcohol and carbon dioxide gas. This was the spark that officially lit the fire of the 1995 vintage.

၆၆၁

By late morning, things were rolling along, and we were in a groove. We were keeping up with the pickers, and the fruit was moving efficiently through the cellar. Then the Cuisinart suddenly lurched, and the conveyer slowed down, and within seconds it all came to a grinding halt. The electricity had died.

Peter cried out, "Noooo bueno!"

It could have been something as simple as the generator running out of diesel, but I knew that wasn't the case, as Bill would have never started an important day like this without a full tank of gas.

Richard immediately started messing with the breaker panel that was located in the tiny bathroom adjacent to the lab. We all gathered around Richard, the canyon's god of electricity, as he started yanking on breaker switches and wires. Our crowded hovering in the bathroom doorway must have been making Bill nervous, because he said, "Clear out, boys, and make yourselves busy."

There wasn't much we could do. Zinfandel fruit was sitting idle on the dumper and the conveyer. The Cuisinart was full, too. It wasn't a good situation. You didn't want the fruit to just be sitting there getting warm in the open air. You wanted it to remain cool, and you wanted to get it into the fermenter efficiently with minimal air exposure. Otherwise, it became prone to "oxidation," resulting in inferior wine.

Even worse, the yellowjackets started swarming around in force, attracted by the sweet, immobile fruit. The western yellowjacket is a predatory wasp with bright yellow and black markings. The adult worker males come out in force by midsummer. Early in their lifecycle, they are most attracted to protein foods, such as meat, fish and pet food scraps. Toward fall, their appetites shift toward sugary fare, which would include fat clusters of Zinfandel sitting out in the open.

The biggest problem at the moment, however, was the winery's derelict electrical system. The wires were undersized and convoluted. They could barely handle the current, and sometimes they just crapped out from the stress. Additionally, the winery's permanent generator was underpowered for handling all of the crush equipment, so Bill had to bring in a supplementary generator. The upside of the second generator was that it added power. The downside was that it would sometimes cause electrical surges.

Thankfully, this time, Richard was seemingly able to identify and patch the problem fairly quickly. We all huddled around the bathroom doorway again. Bill flipped the breakers back. Then, as suddenly as if Richard himself had thrown a thunderbolt from the heavens, the conveyer started rolling and the Cuisinart began whirring. We were back in business.

By now, however, the yellowjackets were feeling pretty cocky, and they paid no heed to the returning humans. Peter was the first casualty.

"Aghhh...Son of a..."

He started flailing around, slapping at his left forearm. The offending insect tumbled over and he stomped it into the cellar floor.

After the clusters were piled into the picking bins, then dumped and raked onto the conveyer, some grapes would inevitably split open, leaking juice onto everything they touched. Pretty soon, we were all walking yellowjacket bait, and as the day warmed up, it only got worse.

I learned that there was only one way to avoid getting stung, and that was to just get into a zen mode and let the little buggers crawl all over you, which was easier said than done. They tickled as they strutted across your skin, their stingers ever ready as they slurped up the grape juice off the hairs on your arm. You had to resist the urge to flinch. If you tried to slap or shake them off, they would just come back angry.

The zen method wasn't foolproof. Every so often, a yellowjacket would sting you just for giggles, but overall it worked. Peter, though, struggled with the zen method. He just hated the things and they made him jumpy. Not surprisingly, he got stung the most. In fact, he later set a Saucelito Canyon record by absorbing 14 stings in one day. Later that night, his heartbeat got erratic, and he had a throbbing in his neck. He thought he might die, but he woke up the next morning in good shape, the toxins having finally worked their way through his system.

The first day of the crush ended quietly. The picking was done by early afternoon, and by late afternoon we had processed all of the fruit and cleaned off the equipment. The yellowjackets retreated as we washed the last of the sticky grape residue down the cellar drain. We joked around and still felt fresh. The crush was off to a good start.

Many harvest days ahead would begin like this one, but they would become progressively more complicated as the weeks wore on. As fermentation space became tight, the small cellar would begin to resemble a chess match, with Bill figuring out where to make his next move. As different lots finished fermentation, we would have to rack the new wine to barrels. We would also have to shovel the skins out of the tanks and press them to liberate the remaining wine.

As these additional tasks were layered into our workflow, the days would start looping around in multiple directions, often concluding long after sundown. For now, we would take as many linear days as we could get.

⚬

After the upper Old Block was picked on October 6, Luis and his crew picked the lower Old Block the next day. The House Block followed shortly thereafter. By mid October, things were really rolling in the cellar.

As the days went by and the crush gathered momentum, the aromas of fermentation began to envelop the property. The smell of fermenting red wine is magnificent. It hovers between sour and sweet, but it is neither. It is pungent, almost feline, and unlike anything else.

Picking, sorting and de-stemming were the appetizer of the crush. Fermentation was the entrée. It was the heart of the matter, the pivot point between the vineyard and the barrel.

Fermentation is fundamentally primal. Ancient peoples happily discovered thousands of years ago that yeasts in the natural environment can spontaneously convert fruit sugars into ethanol (alcohol) and carbon dioxide. In modern winemaking, you can still choose to allow the natural yeasts from the vineyard to initiate fermentation. In most cases, however, commercialized yeasts are used to bring more control and predictability to the process.

When making a red wine like Zinfandel, fermentation takes place in the presence of the grape skins and seeds. This skin contact sets the tone for the resulting wine, as much of the wine's color, flavor and tannin structure is derived from the skins. As the yeasts go to work, the grape juice bubbles and froths and warms up. The skins begin to break down, and the juice—now wine—begins to darken. At this stage, the new wine is cloudy, and it tastes rough and angular and spritzy.

At Saucelito Canyon, fermentation took place in two types of vessels—plastic 4x4-foot bins that could be moved around with a pallet jack, and a fixed open-top 3,000-gallon stainless steel tank behind the winery building.

During fermentation, the grape skins float to the top of the mass, forming a cap that will dry out if left unattended. To foster the desired skin contact, you need to make sure that the skins stay moist and mixed with the juice during fermentation. This is where "punchdowns" and "pumpovers" come into play.

To perform punchdowns at Saucelito Canyon, we stood on the edge of one of the plastic bins, wielding a wooden paddle and punching it through the thick cap. We worked our way around the entire bin, mashing away. By the end, the hard cap had been turned into a supple wet stew. Each bin was punched down two to three times per day. Sore legs and arms were inevitable after a day of punchdowns.

The stainless steel tank out back was too large for punchdowns. In this larger vessel, the new cap was just too hard and thick for a person to mash. Hence the pumpover. With the pumpover, we pumped juice from a valve at the bottom of the tank and out through a hose at the top of the tank to moisten and mix the skins.

Typically, pumpovers are done from some fixed position by securing the hose to a sprinkler at the top of the tank, or at least aiming it from the security of an adjoining catwalk.

But not at Saucelito Canyon. To perform pumpovers on the large open-top tank, we would climb up on the retaining wall behind the tank, then scramble onto a loose board that straddled the top of the tank. We would do our pumpovers while balancing on this board, directly over the wide mouth of grape skins below, the hose bucking in our hands like an angry snake as the juice splashed out of the end.

Abundant carbon dioxide gas is created during fermentation, and with a larger tank the gas and alcohol fumes can be pretty potent. So while we were balancing on the board and steadying the bucking hose with both hands, we were also trying to make sure we weren't getting too light-headed from oxygen deprivation.

You had to get used to the gaseous atmosphere, and you had to know your limits. If one of us had become too light-headed and lost our balance and fallen in when no one was looking, we could have easily croaked. But we didn't, because we managed to observe rule number one: Don't fall in.

"You know," Bill said to a wide-eyed Clarence as he was wrestling with the pumpover hose one afternoon. "I had a friend whose family owned a winery in Santa Barbara, and one of their cellar workers was doing a pumpover one night, and he slipped. The next morning, they fished him out." He drew a forefinger across his neck for emphasis.

That was Bill's version of a safety meeting.

∽◯◯◞

"BOOM!"

A week into the crush, as we were toiling away in the cellar, the background noise of the FM radio was shattered by a shotgun blast in close proximity.

"Holy crap!" Peter hollered, jumping off the forklift. "What was that?"

We were all on edge, our heads swiveling around, trying to figure out what happened. Then we saw Bill's 12-year-old son Tom step out of the lab, white as a ghost, his eyes as big as saucers. Thankfully, he wasn't hurt. Bill put his arm around Tom and took him aside, and the rest of us went back to work.

We soon learned that Tom had been loading his shotgun in the lab, getting ready to poach some vermin, when it slipped in his hand and the trigger got accidentally pulled. He'd had the barrel pointed up and away, so at least that part of his loading procedure went right. The shot went into the ceiling, grazing and denting the elevated water heater on its way up. By the end of harvest, it was just one of many new scars that the winery would wear for years to come.

In the winemaking community, stories of winery accidents are plentiful, but typically only shared in hushed, and sometimes reverent, tones.

At Kenwood Vineyards, I'd personally seen a 600-pound barrel of wine fall from atop a high barrel stack as it was being forklifted out, the thick head of the barrel blowing open as it crashed to the ground, evacuating 60 gallons of wine in mere seconds. If it had landed on someone, they would have been instantly maimed or killed.

Bill relayed the story of a friend who'd clipped the locking lever on a tank manhole with the back of his forklift. The manhole broke open and the entire tank of wine spilled onto the floor as the crew stood there helpless to stop it. Adding insult to injury, the tank "beer canned," or caved in, as the wine evacuated and sucked the air out of the otherwise sealed vessel.

There was the story of a cellar worker at a large winery who spent hours pumping wine out of a tank in the cellar to another vessel outside, only to discover that he'd forgotten to hook the hose up at the far end. He'd reportedly vomited when he realized what he'd done. I'd heard about a Napa Valley winery whose crew had absentmindedly pumped a bunch of white wine into a tank full of the winery's precious premium Cabernet Sauvignon. Not far from Saucelito Canyon, a worker at a local winery had been injured when he accidentally opened the gate on a full tank, only to find himself pinned against the wall by a flood of sweet Muscat Canelli.

Then there were the more gruesome stories. People had caught their arms in steel augurs. They had been maimed in forklift accidents, run over by vineyard tractors, drowned in reservoirs, and perished after falling into tanks.

You're going to have stories like this in any industry with lots of moving parts and heavy machinery. But when you throw in the fatigue and sleep deprivation of the crush, the chances of something going wrong only escalate.

Thankfully, the biggest wound inflicted by the 1995 crush at Saucelito Canyon was the one to the water heater.

Chapter Eight

FAITHFULNESS

DESPITE OUR FOLLIES and antics, there was a thread of reverence that ran through all of us on the Saucelito Canyon cellar crew. There was a sense that we were helping make something of significance, and we were dutiful in that responsibility. We knew when to stop goofing off and start grinding away.

Every so often, we would open a bottle of Saucelito Canyon Zinfandel at the end of the workday to remind us why we were there. This place had earned a reputation for producing some of California's finest Zinfandel, and it was our job to uphold that reputation.

In wine, as mentioned earlier, there is the concept of *terroir*, a French term that signifies how the influence of

113

place—soil, topography, weather—shapes and defines a wine. Terroir is what elevates wine beyond a mere recipe or a commodity like a can of soup.

But at Saucelito Canyon, it was impossible to separate the natural place from the human circumstances. From my vantage, you couldn't talk about the terroir of Bill's wine without factoring in the people and the culture from which it originated.

For example, it would have been ideal to ferment all of the Zinfandel lots in the small 4x4 bins. Fermentations were easier to control in the small bins. But because of space and labor limitations, we also needed to use the large open-top fermenter out back. Unlike most fermentation tanks, however, this one wasn't refrigerated—it had a cooling jacket, but Bill didn't have a coolant delivery system. This tank was a hand-me-down from another winery. It fit the space and the budget, and so there it was.

From a textbook standpoint, the fermentations in this tank got way too hot, sometimes exceeding 100 degrees, with no way to cool it down. But here's the thing: Bill found that he liked it. If he hadn't liked it, he would have done something about it. But he felt that the added heat extracted more flavor from the skins. There were downsides, like the perpetual threat of "stuck" fermentations if the heat caused the yeasts to shut down. There was also the risk of the high temperatures extracting an elevated amount of astringent compounds from the skins and seeds.

Would you have wanted to ferment all of the wine like this? No. But fermenting a portion of the wine like this brought something different to the final blend. This hot fermentation became part of the annual fabric of Bill's Zinfandel, an added dimension that had nothing to do with the land or the weather, and everything to do with the circumstances and culture of the winery. Bill was comfortable with it, and so that's how it went down—textbooks be damned.

When it comes to wine, there's a fine line between subtle flaws and charming quirks. For example, many French wines are distinguished by the presence of brettanomyces, or "brett," which is largely regarded in American winemaking as a spoilage organism. Brett brings a certain funk to a wine, and it can easily get out of hand if left unchecked. But as a professor at the esteemed UC Davis winemaking school once noted, "There's no denying that brett is part of many wines' regional character."

So if you eradicated all of the brett from these French wines, would you be correcting a flaw—or eliminating a charm?

The same type of question could have been asked about the too-hot fermentations and other textbook-defying methods that were specific to the culture and circumstances of Saucelito Canyon.

There are many great wines that are technically immaculate, made with the finest equipment in highly controlled environments. But that wasn't the type of great wine Bill was trying to make—because he didn't want to, and because it wasn't possible in the canyon anyways. If you wanted to drink an impeccably polished wine, there were plenty of other options. But if you wanted to drink a wine whose aromas and flavors took you someplace wholly unique, then you couldn't go wrong with a bottle of Saucelito Canyon Zinfandel.

I think the larger question is: should a wine have a soul—can it?—and if so, where does it come from?

By today's standards, our methods and equipment during the 1995 crush would be called primitive. Even at the time, Saucelito Canyon was old school, chock full of equipment that was verging on rinky dink. But as Bill told me some years later, after he had upgraded his crusher-destemmer and press, "Getting better equipment didn't make the wines better, it just made our lives easier."

Bill had proven that he could make remarkable wine in the canyon—not in spite of the circumstances, but rather because of them. This was his element. He had mastered the challenges and turned them into strengths.

So when the rest of us reported for duty each morning, we didn't see the carnival that an outsider might have seen. We knew better. We saw the possibilities, not the limitations. We had tasted the wines. We knew what was possible from this place. We trusted Bill, and we followed him faithfully.

This was our show, and we owned it.

⌒⌒

Bill was twitchy during the first week of the crush. He would draw juice samples from the Cuisinart, and later from the fermenters, and scuffle off to the lab to run the numbers. He would also sometimes draw the new wine into a glass, then sniff and sip it quietly before returning back to the lab or the Prowler without a word. He was evaluating things, and he wasn't tipping his hand.

The rest of us weren't experienced enough to tell where the 1995 vintage was headed, at least not this early in the game. Fermenting wine is a strange warm brew of alcohol, sweetness, spritziness and yeastiness. But a seasoned winemaker can see through the strangeness, and can decipher a direction through the colors, aromas and flavors that are beginning to take shape. We wondered: What was Bill seeing? How were we doing? He wasn't saying.

During the final rounds of punchdowns on the initial Old Block lots, I could see the color of the juice deepening by the day. The aromas became less gaseous and angular. It was beginning to smell and look like wine. I was hopeful that it would ultimately reflect well on us, but there was still a long ways to go.

Bill wasn't one for chitchat. When he did speak during the workday, it was usually just a quick nudge for the betterment of the wine. He would remind us to be extremely thorough when cleaning the tanks, and to dig deep when doing punchdowns. He would tell us to rake the fruit gently onto the sorting conveyer, lest we unnecessarily split the grapes open. He wasn't the type of leader who screamed at you when you were doing something wrong. He would simply make a suggestion, empowering and inspiring you to do the right thing.

Bill didn't scream at his wine, either. By that, I mean that he let things play out. If something was funky with a given lot, he wouldn't freak out and immediately intervene. He seemed ever mindful of Newton's third law: "For every action, there is an equal and opposite reaction." He wasn't eager to take action and change the natural course of the wine. Sometimes, a wine just needed time to work out the kinks on its own.

Wine is a living thing, and like all of us it goes through awkward moments and growth spurts and rebellious phases. Bill understood this, and so he gave his wines a long leash. It wasn't always easy. Every so often, they would betray his faithfulness. But much more often than not, it's just what they needed.

Chapter Nine

UN-MANAGEMENT

OUR COLLECTIVE ENERGY began to drag by mid October. The hours were piling up, and the dry harvest sun continued to redden our necks. Some fermentations were just starting, others were finishing, and now the additional task of pressing the wine was straining our manpower. On top of that, the Winery Block still needed to be picked and processed. As Bill had predicted, things were getting hairy, and competing needs were colliding.

That's when James came onto the scene. I first learned about James when Bill passed me a note that Nancy had taken. There was a telephone number at the top. Below the number, she'd written: "James Pile-of-Feces."

"Pile-of-Feces?" I said

"Yeah, this guy, James, heard there might be some work out here," Bill said. "He called, and Nancy picked up. She asked him to spell his full name, I guess it was Greek or something. Long name. He told her, 'My buddies just say Pile-of-Feces.'"

Bill said that he'd called the guy back and told him he could come out tomorrow. It was good timing. We were now in the thick of the crush. Peter was increasingly late, and occasionally truant. We were all fatigued. It was a good time to bring a warm body off the bench.

"What time will he be here?" I asked.

Bill just shrugged his shoulders.

Such was life in the Saucelito Time Zone. Bill practiced what I called un-management. Things like time and human resources were exceedingly flexible in the canyon. I sensed that Bill relished the randomness of it all, the "not knowing" of who might show up, of what the day might bring.

All Bill was doing, really, was following Mother Nature's own unpredictable lead. She could send heat, rain or even fire our way at any moment, and we would just have to roll with it. Every single day in the vineyard was really just a link in a long chain of randomness that would shape the eventual wine. A marine layer that hangs around for an extra few hours. A sudden spike in the afternoon temperature. An unusually cold morning. A drizzling fog. These were the cards dealt daily from Mother Nature's own un-ending deck.

In the words of Hamlet, Bill's un-management method was simply "to hold, as 'twere, the mirror up to nature."

Therefore, like the sun and the fog, the heat or a breeze, James would arrive when he arrived, if he arrived at all.

☙

By 9 a.m. the following day, we were already two hours into the shift, and it was still just Bill and me. I was getting pissed. Even I had my limits when it came to un-management. I didn't have the luxury of not showing up. I lived at the place. I had nowhere to run, and nowhere to hide. I felt that some of the others were abusing their freedom.

Richard couldn't arrive until midday. Adam wasn't available, and neither was Clarence. That left us counting on Peter, as well as James. Would either of them show?

Suddenly, over the rattle of the crusher, came the rumble of a motorcycle.

"Gotta be James!" Bill yelled.

We had just finished emptying a bin of grapes. Bill filled a beaker full of fresh grape juice from the crusher and took it into the lab to record its vitals. I pulled the empty bin back down onto the dumper, then hopped on the forklift.

As I backed out of the cellar, I saw James, who was parking his shiny black motorcycle. He was tall and broad-shouldered. I sensed that he was a no-nonsense kind of guy. He probably wasn't going to live and breathe wine-making, but he wasn't going to whine about getting stuck doing punchdowns, either. We could use a guy like that.

I introduced myself.

"So where's Wonder Boy?" he asked.

"Who?"

"Peter."

He explained that he knew Peter from Mr. Rick's tavern in Avila Beach. James was a bartender there, and Peter was a regular. It was all starting to make sense. So that's how James had heard about Saucelito Canyon...

"We don't know where he is," I said.

James laughed. He said, "Well he wasn't feeling any pain last night, but he probably is this morning."

Bill walked out and said hello, and led James on a brief tour of the operation. I noticed a cloud of dust on the approach. Peter's truck came flying down the driveway.

I forked another bin and drove it over to the dumper. Peter stood in the cellar doorway, rubbing his eyes.

"Wha's up?" he said.

"Nada, nada, limonada."

"James here?"

"Yeah, he's with Bill. Dude, you look like crap..."

"Whatever," Peter interrupted. "You don't look so hot yourself with that ugly hat."

He wasn't in a good mood. I knew the drill: He would grouse and grumble and shuffle around for about an hour. Then, toward noon, he would get a second wind and become the life of the cellar. After lunch, with some fuel in his gut, he would become an unstoppable force of comedy. He would perform spot-on imitations and tell rowdy jokes. When the last of the grapes tumbled off the conveyor, he would mimic a stewardess, telling us to "please feel free to walk about the cabin" as he went to fetch the next bin. Every crush needs a class clown, and Peter was ours.

"Geez, look at all these freakin' bins!" Peter muttered.

I didn't want to look. There were still four full bins of Winery Block grapes waiting for us, four bins that had stacked up because there had only been two of us to dump, sort and process the fruit all morning.

We rarely kept pace with the pickers, and were always behind by a bin or two. But when the bins stacked up to three, four, five...That's when things could start to go sideways. That's when the wine gods liked to invoke their version of Murphy's Law, which is: Anything that can go wrong, will go wrong precisely when the grape bins are stacking up.

This particular day, however, was still relatively young, and there was still hope that we could pick up the pace and knock out some of those bins before things got out of hand. Peter was dragging, but James could help save the day. Bill's un-management method was working its charms.

Now that we had three bodies to do the physical work, Bill retired to the lab, running juice samples and serving as the winery's nerve center, tending to a fragmented mental database that kept track of everything from yeast inoculations to equipment orders to telephone calls.

Peter grabbed the garden rake and assumed the role of fruit raker and bin dumper. Meanwhile, James and I took our positions on the conveyer. I flipped the switch, and the belt spun forward and Peter slowly raked clusters from the dumper chute onto the conveyer. We ran it for about 30 seconds until the entire belt was covered in grape clusters, then shut it off.

"So what are we looking for?" James asked.

"Well, it's sort of a judgment call," I began.

"This is out of here, eh?" James said, holding up a miserable cluster half-encrusted with black mold.

"Garbage," I said. He pitched it into the waste barrel at our feet.

"But this, this is late harvest," Peter said, lifting up a raisined cluster that was untouched by mold. "We make a dessert wine out of it. Looks like hell, but it makes a bitchin' wine."

He tossed the dried-out cluster into a large plastic pickle barrel that served as the anaerobic fermentation vessel for the Saucelito Canyon Late Harvest Zinfandel, a sweet dessert wine made in very limited quantities.

James picked up another late-harvest candidate and pitched it into the pickle barrel. He was getting the hang of things. It wasn't rocket science.

Once the bin was empty, Peter jumped on the forklift before I could get to it. Forklifting was Peter's favorite activity. Once he got on the thing, you'd have to peel his fingers from the wheel to get him off.

As usual, he piloted the forklift like he was starring in the Dukes of Hazzard, yanking it into high-speed reverse, flying backward off the concrete pad and into the large dirt turnabout, where he would wheel around to pick up one of the bins stacked in the shade of a great oak. Eventually, Bill stepped out of the lab, took a look at Peter on the forklift, and said, "James, you might want to move your motorbike. I've just got that Peter feeling."

James hesitated. His motorbike was parked in the corner of the turnabout. Only the most reckless forklift driver could reach it. Then he took a second look at Peter and must have got that "feeling," too. So he went over to his bike, kicked the stand and walked it all the way back to Bill's Prowler trailer. Now it was not only completely out of the way, but also next to a big immovable object.

When we were done sorting the next bin, Peter hopped on the forklift, scooped up the empty bin and screeched out of the cellar in reverse. The next thing we heard was a loud clang, and then a thud. I glanced nervously at James, and could see the embers of anger alighting in his eyes. No, it couldn't be...We rushed out of the cellar.

There was Peter, beside the idling forklift, sheepishly picking up the motorbike. Bill, who had gone to eat a late lunch inside the Prowler, thrust the trailer's door open, and we exchanged nervous glances.

James' teeth gritted, his eyes narrowed. The longest second of uncertainty hovered in the hot October air. Suddenly, James rushed toward Peter.

"What in the hell were you thinking?" he shouted, jabbing a finger in Peter's chest.

"Oh, man, I'm sorry," Peter said.

An awkward silence ensued. We were all waiting for James' next word or move.

The silence was broken when James finally said the only thing he could really say: "Fuckin'-A, Peter!"

Thankfully, James limited his physical contact to the finger in Peter's chest. Peter obviously felt bad. There was no point in a brawl.

We all surrounded the motorbike, discovering that the damage was surprisingly minimal, confined to a small ding and some scratches. This seemed to further quell James' rage. Once the commotion was over, we all looked back toward the cellar to appreciate just how far Peter had navigated the forklift outside the bounds of any conceivable path. It was so ridiculous that Peter himself didn't try to explain or make excuses. That was just how he rolled on the forklift, like a bat out of hell, and sometimes there was collateral damage.

In the end, James took it pretty well. But his mood was darkened. I realized that our brief honeymoon with James was over. There would be no becoming his buddy to the point of calling him Pile-of-Feces to his face. In fact, I could tell that soon there would be no James at all. He didn't need this. Bartending paid better, and he also made $18 an hour working at the nuclear power plant during the outages. He might return for another day or two, but that would be it.

It turned out I was right. James ultimately became a short blip on Bill's un-management radar, and a small yet memorable part of the 1995 vintage's DNA.

Chapter Ten

TRIAL BY FIRE

IN LOFTIER MOMENTS, you could call winemaking an art. Practically speaking, it's a craft. But toward the end of the crush, there's little time or energy left for elegant thoughts. Your brain is foggy, your spine aches, your hands are scored and stained red, and shit just needs to get done.

At that point, winemaking is neither an art nor a craft, but rather just a monkey on your back. And to get the monkey off your back, you need to plow ahead and press the wine and get it into the barrel.

At the conclusion of fermentation, you have fresh new wine. It doesn't taste like the wine you find in a bottle. It's raw and simple and even a bit spritzy. The only thing it has on its side is time. Much of this new wine can be easily drained from the fermentation vessel, in which case it's called "free-run" juice. Once you remove the free-run juice, you're left with a sopping wet mass of grape skins. This is what needs to be pressed.

Pressing is the act of squeezing the grape skins to liberate extra wine, not unlike wringing a sponge. At Saucelito Canyon, we used a small variation on the classic wooden "basket" press that you see in illustrations of antique winemaking.

The press consisted of a metal trough base that supported a cylindrical basket of upright wooden slats. The pressing action was powered by a hydraulic bladder that ran up through the center of the basket. You dumped the skins into the press, then hooked up a garden hose to the bladder. As the bladder expanded, it pressed the skins outward against the wooden slats. The increasing pressure liberated the liquid from the skins. The liquid flowed downward into the trough and then out a spout at the front.

Once the skins were pressed, we would drain the bladder and unhook the wooden basket, leaving us with a dry "cake" of grape skins that formed a perfect upright circle.

Pressing was no small chore. We had to shovel the wet skins out of the fermentation bins and tanks, one five-gallon bucket at a time. We would carry the heavy buckets over to the press and dump them in. Shovel, carry, dump, return. It was usually a tag-team operation—one guy in the tank with the shovel, the other on the ground hauling buckets. Once the press cycle was over, we would pry the dense grape skin cake apart by hand and shovel, tossing the pieces into a field bin for disposal in the vineyard.

It was hard labor, but bucket by bucket, we slowly made our way toward the finish line of the 1995 crush.

One afternoon, I was walking by the press when I suddenly felt a blast of liquid against my ribs. I looked down at my t-shirt, and it was soaked with red wine all down the side. I looked at the press, and it was just sitting there, wine slowly trickling out of its spout. I swiveled around, looking for Peter, our resident practical joker. But he wasn't around. I couldn't figure it out.

I went about my business, but a few minutes later something caught the corner of my eye: it looked like a stream of liquid had shot out of the press for a half second! There was a telltale trail of red wine on the concrete. I walked over to the press and waited, but it didn't happen again.

Peter came around and laughed when I showed him my shirt. I told him what I saw. Somehow, a small channel must have opened up through the skins in the press, enough for the wine to shoot out a couple of times through the slats in the wood. End of story, or so we thought.

Soon enough, it was time for another press cycle, so we opened up the press and pried the cake apart. Then we reassembled the press and tag-teamed it, with Peter shoveling and me dumping buckets.

We had just started the next press cycle when it happened again. The liquid squirted straight out the side, right before our eyes. A moment later, another stream hit Peter square in the stomach. "Agggh!" he hollered, jumping back.

We fetched Bill. He looked at our stained shirts with a bemused grin. We told him what was happening, and waited for it to happen again. Once it did, Bill just stood there for a second, speechless. Again, he'd seen everything, but he hadn't seen this.

The frequency of the squirting began to accelerate, and soon we had a full-blown crisis on our hands. Bill was at a loss. It turned out that, for some reason, the skins weren't compressing like normal this year. We couldn't let it keep happening at this rate, but what were we going to do?

We scratched our heads and discussed our options. It was sounding grim until Bill alighted on a possible solution: shrink wrap.

During bottling, once we had a pallet full of case boxes, we wrapped them tight for a safe journey to the warehouse. What if we did the same thing with the press to contain the squirting?

Off I went to grab a roll of leftover wrap from the shop. Peter held the loose end against the press until I made a full circle. I made several more passes until the entire press was wrapped as tight as a mummy. Then we waited.

What happened next made us howl with laughter. As the first squirt opened up, it hit the plastic and tried in vain to find a clear channel, making a distinct farting noise as it was forced into the folds of the plastic. Victory! The liquid was contained. It could only flow one way now: down.

This was the "Saucelito Way" in its purest form: ingenuity mixed with comedy to achieve a successful result. It didn't take us long to come up with a name for our invention. We called it the "Intergalactic Prophylactic Press." It served us well for the remainder of the crush.

In the mid morning of October 26, Peter was the first to notice a puff of dark smoke that was trailing up from behind the ridgeline to the southeast.

Bill took it in stride. "I heard there was going to be a controlled burn near Huasna," he said.

Soon, however, the puff grew into a plume, and then the plume grew into roiling black clouds that darkened the horizon.

"Don't worry children, it's all under control!" Peter hollered.

Within an hour, smoke started blowing our way, casting a thick pall overhead. Next, a California Department of Forestry fire bomber flew right over the vineyard.

"That's all for show!" Peter said. "Remember, it's all under control."

Bill disappeared into the Prowler, where he kept his law enforcement scanner. He stepped out a few minutes later and declared, "Apparently, it's no longer technically a controlled burn."

More CDF aircraft roared over the vineyard. Ashen smog settled into the canyon, stinging our eyes and throats. The fire was still at least a few miles away. But the temperature was 82 degrees, a warm breeze was blowing, and the chaparral by nature was always itching to burn.

"I've got a great idea," Peter said. "Let's wait until late fall, so that everything's nice and crispy. Then, when the weather forecast calls for temps in the eighties with a stiff breeze, we light the fuckin' forest on fire and try to contain it. Sound like a plan?"

Bill grabbed his scanner from the Prowler and rummaged around the lab for some topographic maps. We all hopped on the Mule and drove it up to the fire trail vista, but we couldn't see the fire behind the thick wall of smoke.

The canyon had never burned during Bill's time there, but one day, someday, it inevitably would. He had to be wondering if today might be the day.

We listened intently to the scanner. At one point, one of the spotter planes called in an area for one of the bombers to target. There was a brief silence before the bomber replied,

"What the..." Another pause. The spotter replied: "Disregard." Bill perused his topographical map. "Good thing they balked," he said. "The spotter would have steered them right into the mountain."

We returned to the winery, but Bill kept his ear close to the scanner. By around 3 p.m. the threat dissipated. The smoke began to clear. The fire seemed to have changed direction, or at least slow down. We carried on with our winemaking business.

The local paper ran a big story the following day headlined: "Planned brush fire races out of control." We learned that the CDF had intended to steadily burn 1,400 acres. But about a quarter of the way through the operation, the flames got away from them. Fire engines from six cities were pressed into action. A total of seven planes and two helicopters also joined the fight.

It took until 6 p.m. for them to get the upper hand, but not until 2,900 acres had burned, and not until Bill got nearly his biggest scare of the season, second only to his son shooting the water heater.

༄

The day grew long as we fell into our daily rhythm of shoveling, dumping, pressing and punching down.

We were still at it after the sun went down. By around 9 p.m., we were on the home stretch. I found myself entangled in a knot of pumps, hoses, buckets, valve fittings and flashlights. It's at such moments that a cellar rat—wet, exhausted and cross-eyed—might be inclined to indulge in the forbidden fruit of winemaking: laziness. It was the inclination to skip that last punchdown, to leave some fittings on the ground for tomorrow, to do a half-assed job of rinsing the pumps—and to ultimately make a half-assed wine. The forbidden fruit was tempting, but we always managed to resist it.

The moon was out, yellowed by the lingering smoke. I heard Peter approaching on the tractor, returning from dumping a bin of pressed grape skins in the vineyard. He pulled up quickly and brought the tractor to a halting skid.

"Listen," he said, his eyes flickering with excitement. "There's a coyote in the vineyard, ripped to shreds, dead, blood all over. Something nasty's out there."

We hopped onto the Mule, picked up Peter's dog, grabbed the 12-gauge from the cottage and motored up to the murder scene.

"Geez, Peter," I said when we arrived. "That thing's been dead for a month."

It was the same old coyote that I'd been watching slowly decompose on my bird-control rounds. Peter shrugged his shoulders. I could see how he'd been duped. The coyote was still partly intact, and next to it were spilled grape skins that had been jostled loose from an earlier dump run.

In the imperfect light of the hazy moon, I could see how the scene might have looked gruesome from a distance, the dark grape skins trailing from the carcass like bloody entrails.

We returned to the winery, flushed the hoses, deconstructed the pumps, washed the buckets and press, hosed the concrete down, and drank a few Lone Stars.

It would be one of our last nights like this. The vineyard had been picked clean, and the last lots were now finishing fermentation. After another several days of pressing and barreling down, the crush would be over and the final cleanup would begin.

After Peter drove off, I turned up the radio and started the final round of punchdowns. Once that was done, I shut off the generator and closed the sliding cellar door. Watching the door meet the frame and hearing that soft thud of wood on wood always seemed like a small miracle. It signified the end of yet another day that seemed like it might never end.

During the last days of the crush, I felt dog tired on the outside, but awakened on the inside. The experience was grueling yet transformative. The cottage had become my home, and the canyon my universe. I was hardly Thoreau at Walden Pond, but this was my own version of it.

As a person, I felt stronger and more alert and more appreciative. My outlook had been sharpened by Bill's unspoken sermons of self-reliance and devotion to the task. The achievement of helping grapes become wine was tangible and finite, and something to be proud of.

In the end, we had processed 30 tons of grapes. Each cluster had been hand sorted. Every grape skin had been shoveled out of the fermentation vessels and carried to the press in five-gallon buckets. All of the wine had been racked to individual 60-gallon barrels.

The barrels were crammed into all corners of the small winery building. Getting them rinsed, filled and back into the cellar on stacked barrel racks had been no easy task.

By the end of October, the Indian summer was wobbling on its last legs. The sun was finally tuckered out, and the cooler temperatures were a relief. On the afternoon of Halloween, we found ourselves stacking the last of the barrels.

Bill walked out of the lab carrying a couple of glasses and a wine thief—a glass tube used for drawing wine out of a barrel. He squeezed himself into the back of the tight stacks and came out carrying a few glasses of wine. It was wine from the upper Old Block, the first block that had been picked 25 days earlier.

We gathered around and sniffed and sipped the new wine. It was still young and rough, but clearly pointed in the right direction. The color was dark purple at the core, and crimson at the ridges. Aromas of dusty red fruit jumped out of the glass. Somewhere, the ghost of Henry Ditmas was smiling.

Bill was smiling, too. "Boys," he said, "We did it."

Chapter Eleven

THE FINAL HOWL

EVERY FIRST WEEKEND in November, the local vintners' association held a harvest celebration, with a grand tasting on Saturday, and winery open houses on Sunday.

It was all hands on deck for the Saucelito Canyon open house. Nancy and the kids, Tom and Margaret, were there. Peter, Richard and Clarence showed up, along with some other friends of the Greenough family.

My buddy Mike Sinor also came out to lend a hand. We had become fast friends while working together at a local tasting room three years earlier, and he had gone on to work the 1993 crush at Saucelito Canyon. Mike's experience in the canyon had ignited a fascination with winemaking, ultimately driving him to become one of the Central

Coast's most skilled winemakers. His was one of many lives changed by working the crush with Bill.

Quite a few people made the trek out to the canyon for the open house. We poured wine and served appetizers and answered questions about the wines and vineyard. By late afternoon, the traffic dwindled, and at around 4 p.m. we cleaned up for good.

Daylight savings time had just ended, and it was getting dark early. Long shadows crept over the winery, and the temperature plummeted as the sun ducked behind the mesa. But we all hung around. There was much to celebrate, not just the end of another long day, but the conclusion of another crush in the canyon.

Glasses of wine were poured. A few Lone Stars were cracked. Bill broke out one of his precious bottles of seep.

We cranked up Don Walser—the Yodeling Cowboy—on the winery boombox. We all whooped and hollered when Walser's "Rolling Stone from Texas" came on. It was funny not only because Bill disliked Texas, but also because Walser unleashes the mother of all yodels on that song. Nancy got up and started doing a crazy two-step. The kids really got a kick out of seeing their mother let loose, and we all joined in.

The mirthfulness was accentuated by a collective sense of relief. We'd had plenty of fun during the crush, but it had also been intense. We were all drained by the end.

Now it was over, our work was done. Maybe there was even a hint of sadness in the air, in the knowing that it was done.

On every morning of the crush, you woke up early with a sense of purpose. The mission was clearly defined and all consuming, and it made life simple. Then, suddenly, the mission was accomplished, and you couldn't help but wonder: "What now?"

That was the question that gnawed at the edges of this festive evening. But this was no time to dwell on it. This was a time to party, and party we did.

Bill and Nancy were too polite to tell me to leave, but I knew it was time.

We spent a week doing final cleanup. The sorting conveyor, Cuisinart, picking bins and wine press were now all tucked away in the pole barn. All of the winery floors and walls had been pressure washed. The vines were starting to drop their leaves and would soon go dormant for the winter.

It was hard to believe, but there was nothing else to be done. The new vintage was resting in the barrels. The barrels would need to be monitored, but Bill would do that. After all of the harvest bustle, the sudden quiet in the canyon was almost eerie.

From late August through the post-harvest days of early November, I averaged 60 hours of work per week, and neared 80 hours per week several times in the heat of the crush. During the middle week of November, however, I logged 37 hours. The following week, it was just 24 hours. The writing was on the wall.

On my second-to-last morning in the canyon, I found the remains of our dead coyote mounted on a fencepost, its mouth frozen in a silent howl directed at the heavens. I figured that Bill must have stuck it on the post before he went home the previous evening. He later denied doing it, but there were no other suspects.

I thought of it as the perfect scarecrow for wine snobs. Bill hated wine snobs. Not that any wine snobs ever came out to the canyon, but if they did...well, this would surely scare them off.

The next day, I packed up my truck. It didn't take long. Once again, my cat rode shotgun. On my way out, I saluted the dead coyote. In the rear-view mirror was an experience of a lifetime. In front of me was a long dirt road, going somewhere.

Chapter Twelve

FULL CIRCLE

BILL LEFT SANTA Barbara in 1974, and I left Santa Cruz County in 1995, but we both ended up at the same place, each at the right time. The canyon had set Bill free. Twenty-one years later, it had pulled me together.

We were both the better for it, and that was how we found ourselves at the end of the crush. Bill was living his dream, and he had given me the opportunity to consider mine.

The pay was low, but I'd still built up a bit of a nest egg during the crush, because I'd had no time or place to spend my paychecks on anything else but food and Lone Star. After I left Saucelito Canyon, I landed a caretaker-for-rent gig in Pebble Beach. With no overhead and my little nest egg, I was able to buy some time and finally put my college degree to use, carving out a living as a freelance journalist. This eventually set me up for related work in media relations, and today I run a marketing consultancy with my wife. In many ways, who I am and what I do today are rooted in that fateful autumn in the canyon.

I still think about the World War II veterans who inspired a young Bill Greenough with their can-do spirit and entrepreneurial undertakings. I think about the counter-cultural visionaries on Mountain Drive who took Bill under their wing and introduced him to the gift of wine. I think about all of the dominos that fell from those experiences, prompting Bill to embark on his own improbable adventure. And I think about Bill's son Tom, who now towers over the both of us. A few years ago, Bill turned the winemaking reins over to Tom, and now the next generation is writing its own stories in the canyon.

At the center of it all remains a three-acre block of Zinfandel vines planted in 1880 by an adventurous Englishman. When Henry Ditmas left the canyon, divorced and perhaps driven out in 1886, he may have felt like a failure. If only he could witness his unlikely legacy. If only he could know that it wasn't for naught, and that many lives have been changed by the very vines he planted, vines that are still producing wine more than 130 years later.

On paper, the 1995 crush didn't look so hot. When you have to shrink-wrap your press just to make it through the season, you've flown well beyond the orbit of perfect-world winemaking.

But in the bottle, we were golden. After the 1995 Zinfandel Estate was released, the *Wine Spectator* gave it a resounding score of 92 points, praising it as "multidimensional" and "complex."

At the end of the day, we were measured by what we made, not how we made it. We couldn't ask for more.

⟨∞⟩

Now here I was, so many years later, at the anniversary tasting in the canyon. We'd produced exactly 2,222 cases of 1995 Zinfandel, or 26,664 bottles. Very few of these bottles remained in existence, and one had just been opened and poured into my glass.

I worked up the nerve to smell the old wine, and to take a sip. The 1995 Zinfandel had shed the youthful vibrancy I remembered. It was a little creaky at the joints and pointing toward the downward slope, but still sufficiently structured and defiant. It was wiser now, its fruit yielding to earthier nuances that spoke even more vividly to the surrounding chaparral. Like the vines it came from, this wine was a survivor.

The crowd settled in. A local trio was playing folk music, and food was plentiful. Dusk was settling into the canyon. The canes of the old vines swayed in the warm breeze.

Bill seemed to be having a great time. He had earned it.

I looked over at my three-year-old son, who was playing around with rocks and sticks and other fascinating things from the vineyard, and dirtying himself in the same soil that I had toiled in many years ago. I took another sip. The wine was still alive. It still told a story, a story that my boy might enjoy someday, I thought.

I went home that night, dusted off my old notes and memories, cracked a bottle of wine, and started writing.

ACKNOWLEDGMENTS

THIS BOOK IS dedicated to Bill and the Greenough family, for an adventure to remember; to Martin J. Smith and Buz Bezore (R.I.P.), two editors who gave an untested young writer a chance following the 1995 crush; to my mother Gay, for her unwavering support; and to my wife Malei and son Easton, my true loves.

Catching Up

Inevitably, the equipment and methods at Saucelito Canyon have been modernized over the years. Second-generation vintners Tom and Margaret Greenough are now taking the helm of the vineyard and winery operations, while Bill and Nancy also remain deeply involved.

Peter works in security. Richard is a semi-retired aerospace engineer. Clarence is a property manager. All of them still live in San Luis Obispo County.

The places featured in this book—Arroyo Grande Valley, Edna Valley, Paso Robles and Santa Barbara County—are today ranked among the world's premier winemaking regions.

Thanks

Everyone I contacted about this book was unfailingly helpful and gracious. Peter, Richard and Clarence were good sports and remarkably supportive. Stefanie Collins nailed the cover design with amazing grace. Chris Leschinsky generously shared the telling photo that graces the back cover. Mike Sinor helped keep the creative flame burning all these years. Rob DaFoe delivered awesome videography as well as ongoing artistic inspiration. The North County book club (you know who you are!) provided early support and helpful feedback. Michael Peake, Ziggy Peake, Elias Chiacos and the Neely family answered my out-of-the-blue phone calls with unquestioning hospitality. The Mountain Drive spirit is alive and well.

Special thanks to Don Dokken for sharing his kind words. In addition to being a heavy metal legend and a pioneer of the iconic Los Angeles hard rock scene, he is a true wine connoisseur. I've been a longtime fan, so his endorsement means a lot to me. For info and upcoming tour dates, check out DokkenCentral.com.

Resources

Two magnificent books provided invaluable historical insight— *Mountain Drive: Santa Barbara's Bohemian Community* by Elias Chiacos; and *Wild Bill Neely and The Pagan Brothers' Golden Goat Winery* by William L. Neely and edited by Allan Shields.

Online

Video of the vineyard and more information can be found at TheMadCrush.com